Stylish Academic Writing

Stylish Academic Writing

Helen Sword

HARVARD UNIVERSITY PRESS
Cambridge, Massachusetts & London, England
2012

Library of Congress Cataloging-in-Publication Data

Sword, Helen.
  Stylish academic writing / Helen Sword.
    p. cm.
  Includes bibliographical references and index.
  ISBN 978-0-674-06448-5 (alk. paper)
1. Academic writing. 2. English language—Style. I. Title.
  LB2369.S96 2011
  808'.0420711—dc23   2011035339

CONTENTS

PREFACE

For many academics, "stylish academic writing" is at best an oxymoron and at worst a risky business. Why, they ask, should we accessorize our research with gratuitous stylistic flourishes? Doesn't overt attention to style signal intellectual shallowness, a privileging of form over content? And won't colleagues reject as unserious any academic writing that deliberately seeks to engage and entertain, rather than merely to inform, its readers?

In this book, I argue that elegant ideas deserve elegant expression; that intellectual creativity thrives best in an atmosphere of experimentation rather than conformity; and that, even within the constraints of disciplinary norms, most academics enjoy a far wider range of stylistic choices than they realize. My agenda is, frankly, a transformative one: I aim to start a stylistic revolution that will end in improved reading conditions for all. In particular, I hope to empower colleagues who have come to believe—I have heard this mantra again and again—that they are "not allowed" to write a certain way. This book showcases the work of academic writers from across the disciplines who stretch and break disciplinary molds—and get away with it. Not only do they publish in respected peer-reviewed journals and place their books with prestigious presses, but they are lauded by their colleagues for their intellectual rigor and flair.

Far from peddling generic, one-size-fits-all advice, this book encourages readers to adopt whatever stylistic strategies best suit their own skin. Stylish academic writing can be serious, entertaining, straightforward, poetic, unpretentious, ornate, intimate, impersonal, and much in between. What the diverse authors profiled here have in common is a commitment to the ideals of *communication, craft,* and *creativity.* They take care to remain intelligible to educated readers both within and beyond their own discipline, they think hard about both *how* and *what* they write, and they resist intellectual conformity. Above all, they never get dressed in the dark.

STYLE AND SUBSTANCE

I

RULES OF ENGAGEMENT

Pick up any guide to effective writing and what will you find? Probably some version of the advice that Strunk and White offered more than half a century ago in their classic book *The Elements of Style:* always use clear, precise language, even when expressing complex ideas; engage your reader's attention through examples, illustrations, and anecdotes; avoid opaque jargon; vary your vocabulary, sentence length, and frames of reference; favor active verbs and concrete nouns; write with conviction, passion, and verve.[1]

Pick up a peer-reviewed journal in just about any academic discipline and what will you find? Impersonal, stodgy, jargon-laden, abstract prose that ignores or defies most of the stylistic principles outlined above. There is a massive gap between what most readers consider to be good writing and what academics typically produce and publish. I'm not talking about the kinds of formal strictures necessarily imposed by journal editors—article length, citation style, and the like—but about a deeper, duller kind of disciplinary monotony, a compulsive proclivity for discursive obscurantism and circumambulatory diction (translation: an addiction to big words and soggy syntax). E. B. White, that great master of literary style, lets his character Charlotte the spider explain the fine art of sucking the lifeblood from a fly:

"First," said Charlotte, "I dive at him." She plunged headfirst toward the fly.... "Next, I wrap him up." She grabbed the fly, threw a few jets of silk around it, and rolled it over and over, wrapping it so that it couldn't move.... "Now I knock him out, so he'll be more comfortable." She bit the fly. "He can't feel a thing now."[2]

Substitute "reader" for the fly and "academic prose" for the spider's silk, and you get a fairly accurate picture of how academic writers immobilize their victims.

The seeds for this book were sown when, several years ago, I was invited to teach a course on higher education pedagogy to a group of faculty from across the disciplines. Trawling for relevant reading materials, I soon discovered that higher education research journals were filled with articles written in a style that I, trained as a literary scholar, found almost unreadable. At first I blamed my own ignorance and lack of background in the field. However, the colleagues enrolled in my course— academics from disciplines as varied as computer science, engineering, fine arts, history, law, medicine, music, and population health—were quick to confirm my niggling feeling that most of the available articles on higher education teaching were, to put it bluntly, very badly written. Instead of gleaning new insights, we found ourselves trying to make sense of sentences such as this:

> In this study, I seek to identify and analyze stakeholders' basic beliefs on the topic of membership that can be considered in normative arguments on whether to allocate in-state tuition benefits to undocumented immigrants.

Or this:

> Via a symbolic interactionist lens, the article analyses the "identity work" undertaken in order to assert distinctive identities as specialist academic administrators.

Or this (ironically, from an article on improving academic writing):

> Rarely is there an effective conceptual link between the current under-
> standings of the centrality of text to knowledge production and student
> learning and the pragmatic problems of policy imperatives in the name
> of efficiency and capacity-building.[3]

At every turn, we found our desire to learn thwarted by gratuitous educational jargon and serpentine syntax.

Do higher education journals hold a monopoly on dismal
writing, I began to wonder, or are these articles just the tip of a
huge pan-disciplinary iceberg? It didn't take me long to confirm
that similarly turgid sentences can be found in leading peer-
reviewed journals in just about any academic field—not only in
the social sciences but also in humanities disciplines such as history, philosophy, and even my home discipline of literary studies,
where scholars pride themselves on their facility with words. I
asked myself: What exactly is going on here? Are academics being explicitly trained to write abstract, convoluted sentences? Is
there a guidebook for graduate students learning the trade that
says, "Thou must not write clearly or concisely" or "Thou must
project neither personality nor pleasure in thy writing" or "Thou
must display no originality of thought or expression"? Do my
colleagues actually enjoy reading this stuff?

Much has already been written—mostly *by* academics—about
academic discourse in all its disciplinary variety.[4] Notably, however, most of these studies replicate rather than challenge the status quo. For example, in his groundbreaking book *Disciplinary
Discourses: Social Interactions in Academic Writing,* Ken Hyland
examines 1,400 texts from five genres in eight disciplines, providing fascinating insights into how various academic genres (the
footnote, the research letter, the book review, the abstract, and so
forth) construct and communicate disciplinary knowledge. Hyland's own prose style reflects his training as a social scientist,
and specifically as a linguist:

> Such practices cannot, of course, be seen as entirely determined; as
> language users are not simply passive recipients of textual effects,

but the impact of citation choices clearly lies in their cognitive and cultural value to a community, and each repetition helps to instantiate and reproduce these conventions.[5]

Note the passive verb construction *(be seen)*, the disciplinary jargon *(instantiate)*, the preposition-laden phrases (*of* textual effects, *of* citation, *in* their value, *to* a community), the multiple abstract nouns *(practices, recipients, effects, impact, value, community, repetition, convention)*, and the near erasure of human agency. Hyland's discourse *about* disciplinary discourse has itself been shaped by disciplinary conventions that insist academic prose must be bland, impersonal, and laden with abstract language.

Yet common sense tells us otherwise. So, indeed, do the authors of the many excellent academic writing guides already on the market, some of which have been in print for decades. William Zinsser, for instance, identifies "humanity and warmth" as the two most important qualities of effective nonfiction; Joseph M. Williams argues that "we owe readers an ethical duty to write precise and nuanced prose"; Peter Elbow urges academic writers to construct persuasive arguments by weaving together the creative and critical strands of their thinking; Richard A. Lanham offers strategies for trimming lard-laden sentences; Howard S. Becker advises apprentice academics to avoid the temptations of so-called classy (that is, intellectually pretentious) writing; and Strunk and White remind us to think of our reader as "a man floundering in a swamp" who will thank us for hoisting him onto solid ground as quickly as possible.[6] Many academics routinely assign these books to students but ignore their advice themselves, perhaps because such commonsense principles strike them as too generic or journalistic to apply to their own work.

So why do universities—institutions dedicated to creativity, research innovation, collegial interchange, high standards of excellence, and the education of a diverse and ever-changing population of students—churn out so much uninspiring, cookie-cutter prose? In a now classic 1993 *New York Times Book Review* article titled "Dancing with Professors," Patricia Nelson Limerick compares academics to buzzards that have been wired to a branch and conditioned to believe they cannot fly freely even when the wire is finally pulled (an extended metaphor that has to be read in its original context to be fully appreciated). She concludes:

> I do not believe that professors enforce a standard of dull writing on graduate students in order to be cruel. They demand dreariness because they think that dreariness is in the students' best interests. Professors believe that a dull writing style is an academic survival skill because they think that is what editors want, both editors of academic journals and editors of university presses. What we have here is a chain of misinformation and misunderstanding, where everyone thinks that the other guy is the one who demands dull, impersonal prose.[7]

Other explanations range from the sympathetic (stylistic conformity offers a measure of comfort and security in an otherwise cutthroat academic universe) to the sociopolitical (the social organization we work in demands high productivity, which in turn encourages sloppy writing) to the practical (we have to learn appropriate disciplinary discourses somehow, and imitation is the easiest way) to the conspiratory (jargon functions like a secret handshake, a signal to our peers that we belong to the same elite insiders' club) to the flat-out uncharitable (Limerick reminds us that today's professors are the people "nobody wanted to dance with in high school").[8]

The question I want to address here, however, is not so much *why* academics write the way they do but *how* the situation might be improved. Four strands of research inform this book. As a starting point, I asked more than seventy academics from across the disciplines to describe the characteristics of "stylish academic writing" in their respective fields. Their responses were detailed, opinionated, and surprisingly consistent. Stylish scholars, my colleagues told me, express complex ideas clearly and precisely; produce elegant, carefully crafted sentences; convey a sense of energy, intellectual commitment, and even passion;

engage and hold their readers' attention; tell a compelling story; avoid jargon, except where specialized terminology is essential to the argument; provide their readers with aesthetic and intellectual pleasure; and write with originality, imagination, and creative flair.

Next, I analyzed books and articles by more than one hundred exemplary authors recommended to me by their discipline–based peers. Most of these stylish academic writers indeed exemplify the criteria described above. However, I found that they achieve abstract ends such as *engagement, pleasure,* and *elegance* not through mystical displays of brilliance and eloquence (although they are undeniably brilliant and eloquent scholars) but by deploying some very concrete, specific, and transferable techniques. For example, I noted their frequent use of the following:

- interesting, eye-catching titles and subtitles;
- first-person anecdotes or asides that humanize the author and give the text an individual flavor;
- catchy opening paragraphs that recount an interesting story, ask a challenging question, dissect a problem, or otherwise hook and hold the reader;
- concrete nouns (as opposed to nominalized abstractions such as "nominalization" or "abstraction") and active, energetic verbs (as opposed to forms of *be* and bland standbys such as *make, find,* or *show*);
- numerous examples, especially when explaining abstract concepts;
- visual illustrations beyond the usual Excel-generated pie charts and bar graphs (for example, photographs, manuscript facsimiles, drawings, diagrams, and reproductions);
- references to a broad range of academic, literary, and historical sources indicative of wide reading and collegial conversations both within and outside their own fields;
- humor, whether explicit or understated.

Significantly, I confirmed that stylish academic writers employ these techniques not only in their books, which are often targeted at nonspecialist audiences, but also in peer-reviewed articles aimed at disciplinary colleagues.

For the third stage of my research, I assembled a data set of one thousand academic articles from across the sciences, social sciences, and humanities: one hundred articles each from international journals in the fields of medicine, evolutionary biology, computer science, higher education, psychology, anthropology, law, philosophy, history, and literary studies. (For a full account of my sources and research methodology, see the appendix.) This corpus barely scratches the surface of academic discourse in all its rich disciplinary variety. Nevertheless, the articles in my data set provide a compelling snapshot of contemporary scholarship at work. I used them not only to locate real-life examples of both engaging and appalling academic prose but also to drill down into specific questions about style and the status quo. For example, how many articles in each discipline contain personal pronouns (*I* or *we*)? How many open with a story, anecdote, question, quotation, or other narrative hook? How many include unusually high or low percentages of abstract nouns? The answers to these and other questions are summarized in Chapter 2 and elsewhere throughout this book.

Finally, to determine whether the realities of scholarly writing match the advice being given to early career academics, I analyzed one hundred recently published writing guides, most of which address PhD-level researchers or above. The results of that study are described in detail in Chapter 3. In a nutshell, I found that the writing guides offer virtually unanimous advice on some points of style (such as the need for clarity and concision) but conflicting recommendations on others (such as pronoun usage and structure). Academics who aspire to write more engagingly and adventurously will find in these guides no shortage of useful advice and moral support. They will also discover, however, that stylish academic writing is a complex and often contradictory business. As Strunk and White remind us in a passage that is dated in its gendered pronoun usage but timeless in its sentiment:

> There is no satisfactory explanation of style, no infallible guide to good writing, no assurance that a person who thinks clearly will be able to write clearly, no key that unlocks the door, no inflexible rule by which the young writer may shape his course. He will often find himself steering by stars that are disturbingly in motion.[9]

Only by becoming aware of these shifting constellations can academics begin to make informed, independent decisions about their own writing.

Overall, my research maps a scholarly universe in which wordy, wooden, weak-verbed academic prose finds few if any explicit advocates but vast armies of practitioners. The good news is that we all have the power to change the contours of that map, one publication at a time—*if we choose to*. The chapters that follow serve two types of scholarly writers: those who want to produce engaging, accessible prose all the time and those who opt to cross that bridge only occasionally. There will always be a place in the world for the technical reports of the research scientist, the esoteric debates of the analytical philosopher, and the labyrinthine musings of the poststructuralist theorist; each of these genres serves a valuable intellectual purpose and reaches appreciative, albeit restricted, audiences. All academics, however, do need to interact with wider audiences at least occasionally: for example, when describing their work to grant-making bodies, university promotion committees, departmental colleagues, undergraduate students, or members of the nonacademic public. In Part 2, "The Elements of Stylishness," I outline strategies and techniques that can help even the most highly specialized researchers communicate with readers who do not understand their peculiar disciplinary dialect. Although the focus of this book is on stylish academic *writing*, these techniques can be applied with equally good effect to the realm of public speaking.

Of course, no one can ever fully quantify style. Like stylish dressing, stylish writing will always remain a matter of individual talent and taste. Moreover, writing styles vary considerably according to content, purpose, and intended audience; you would not expect to wear the same outfit to Alaska in winter and to Spain in summer, or to a black-tie ball and to a sporting competition. All the same, this book reflects my belief—one based on a substantial body of research evidence—that the fundamental principles of stylish academic writing can indeed be described, emulated, and taught. Perhaps the most important of those principles is self-determination: the stylish writer's deeply held belief that academic writing, like academic thought, should not be constrained by the boundaries of convention. Like Limerick's buzzards, afraid to fly free even though the wires that once held them back had long since been severed, many writers lack the confidence to break away from what they perceive—often mistakenly—as the ironclad rules of their disciplinary discourses. This book empowers academics to write as the most effective teachers teach: with passion, with courage, with craft, and with style.

CHAPTER 2

ON BEING DISCIPLINED

discipline *(n.)*

- A branch of instruction or education; a department of learning or knowledge; a science or art in its educational aspect.
- The order maintained and observed among pupils, or other persons under control or command, such as soldiers, sailors, the inmates of a religious house, a prison, etc.
- Correction; chastisement; punishment inflicted by way of correction and training; in religious use, the mortification of the flesh by penance; also, in a more general sense, a beating or other infliction (humorously) assumed to be salutary to the recipient.[1]

To enter an academic discipline is to *become* disciplined: trained to habits of order through corrections and chastisements that are "assumed to be salutary" by one's teachers. Scholarly commentators have variously alluded to the academic disciplines as "silos," "barricades," "ghettos," and "black boxes," using metaphors of containment that implicitly critique the intellectual constraints imposed by disciplinary structures.[2] Yet disciplinarity remains a robust and even sacred concept. University of California chancellor Clark Kerr is said to have described the mid-twentieth-century research university as "a series of individual faculty entrepreneurs held together by a common grievance over parking," and his censure still rings true six decades later: academics often seem more intent on fencing off and tending their own patches of disciplinary turf than on seeking common ground.[3] Even within disciplines that appear relatively homogeneous to an outsider, scholars may belong to warring subdisciplinary clans that have established and entrenched separate identities marked by distinctive ideologies and idiolects. Sociologist Andrew Abbott compares the "fractal distinctions" between subdisciplines to segmental kinship systems: "A lineage starts, then splits, then splits again. Such systems have a number of important characteristics. For one thing, people know only their near kin well."[4]

Recently, a colleague from my own university's medical school told me that she had decided not to enroll in an interdisciplinary faculty development course because it would be "a waste of time" for her to learn about academic writing from anyone outside the medical profession. Her comment reminded me of a news story that I came across a few years ago involving an unlikely but productive collaboration between medical and nonmedical experts. In 2006, surgeons from the Great Ormond Street Children's Hospital invited a team of Ferrari Formula One pit stop mechanics to observe them at work. The mechanics noted a number of inefficiencies in the surgeons' procedures and recommended some key changes, particularly in the areas of synchronization, communication, and patient relocation. The doctors consequently developed new surgical protocols, forged new lines of communication with nurses and technicians, and even designed a new operating gurney to smooth their young patients' transition between the operating room and intensive care. According to one of the participating surgeons, the surgical unit has been transformed into "a centre of silent precision" where "the complications of operations have been substantially reduced."[5] Academic writing is not brain surgery, of course. However, like surgeons and Formula One mechanics, academics do engage daily in a number of complex and highly specialized operations, and our ability to write effectively about our work requires not only training, commitment, and skill but also a willingness to change, grow, and learn from others.

In an article on "signature pedagogies," education researcher Lee Shulman urges university faculty to look beyond the conventional teaching styles of their own disciplines—the demonstration lab (science), the discussion seminar (humanities), the Socratic dialogue (law), the studio session (fine arts), the clinical round (medicine)—and to borrow ideas from elsewhere: for example, an English professor might encourage students to undertake a "live critique" of each other's work (the fine arts studio model) or a mathematics professor might engage students in a structured discussion of key conceptual issues (the humanities seminar model).[6] Similarly, academic writers can make a conscious effort to question, vary, and augment the signature research styles of their own disciplines—which often embody deeply entrenched but unexamined ways of thinking—by appropriating ideas and techniques from elsewhere. Looking around my university, I can't help noting how many of my most eminent colleagues have earned their academic reputations through interdisciplinary endeavors of one kind or another: the evolutionary psychologist who imports into the domain of comparative linguistics classification methods that he learned from studying zoology; the professor of education whose training as a statistician underpins his meta-analysis of educational research from around the world; the anthropology professor who deliberately weaves together historiographic and anthropological methodologies; the literature professor whose groundbreaking work on the origin of stories draws on extensive readings in the fields of evolutionary biology and psychology.[7] All of these distinguished academics have been well schooled in the norms and expectations of their own disciplines, yet none of them toes a predictable party line.

When I first embarked on the research that underpins this book, I harbored a fantasy that I could map a coherent landscape of disciplinary styles, zooming in on specific regions and making informed pronouncements about their inhabitants: "Anthropologists write like this; computer scientists write like that." By the time I had assembled my initial data set, however—one thousand peer-reviewed articles from sixty-six different journals in ten disciplines across the arts, sciences, and social sciences—I realized that a panoptic overview of signature writing styles across the disciplines would be an impossible task. In the 2003 edition of their book *Academic Tribes and Territories,* Tony Becher and Paul Trowler note that "there are now over 1000 maths journals covering 62 major topic areas with 4500 subtopics," and a similarly daunting set of statistics could be generated for most other major academic fields.[8] Casting my porous nets into various disciplinary waters, I felt less like a mapmaker or surveyor than like a lone fisherman at the edge of a vast and seething ocean.

My choice of disciplines for the study was prompted by a mixture of curiosity, expertise, ignorance, and serendipity. In the sciences, I chose medicine because I wondered whether leading medical journals allow for any variation in writing style, evolutionary biology because the field has produced some dazzlingly engaging popular science writers, and computer science because a colleague in that discipline had pointed me to some examples of intriguingly playful peer-reviewed articles. In the social sciences, I included higher education because I was already familiar with research journals in the field, psychology because of its diversity, and anthropology because of the discipline's long tradition of self-reflective writing about writing. In the humanities, I picked philosophy for the distinctiveness of its style, history because colleagues often claim that "historians are good writers," and literary studies, my own home field. To round the number of disciplines up to ten, I tossed in law, which sits somewhere between the social sciences and humanities and has many unique stylistic features of its own.

In most of the disciplines surveyed, I selected five representative journals—another researcher might well have chosen differently—and downloaded the twenty most recent articles from each journal. After the entire data set had been cataloged by a diligent research assistant, I undertook a detailed analysis of five hundred articles (fifty from each discipline). For the most part, I posed quantitative questions designed to yield unambiguously objective answers, for example: How many authors does each article have? What is the average page length per discipline? How many of the articles use first-person pronouns? What percentage of certain types of words can be found in each article? At times, however, I also ventured into more subjective terrain, as when, working from a detailed rubric, my research assistant and I rated the title and opening sentence of each article as "engaging," "informative," or both. (For more details on my sources, selection criteria, and methodology, see the appendix.)

Predictably, as soon as I started presenting the results of my analysis to colleagues from the ten disciplines surveyed, they noted that if I had chosen articles from *this* anthropology journal or *that* computer science journal, my findings would look very different. I also heard grumbles from academics in fields ranging from nursing, fine arts, and engineering to management studies and tourism, whose disciplinary journals had not been part of my survey sample. Both groups of colleagues—those whose disciplines were represented and those whose disciplines were not—felt that I had somehow neglected *them*, whether by failing to grasp the nuances of their particular field or subfield or by ignoring their discipline altogether. Such responses, of course, miss the point of the exercise. The purpose of this book is not to hold a mirror up to academics and show them what they already know about themselves. Instead, I want to encourage readers to look beyond their disciplinary barricades and find out what colleagues in other fields are up to. Like surgeons who believe they have nothing to learn from pit stop mechanics, academics who think they have nothing to learn from researchers outside their own discipline risk missing out on one of the greatest pleasures of scholarly life: the opportunity to engage in stimulating conversations, forge intellectual alliances, and share ideas with people whose knowledge will nurture and stimulate our own.

My data analysis confirmed some disciplinary stereotypes and upended others (see Figure 2.1). For example, I had anticipated

	Personal pronouns	Unique or hybrid structure	Engaging title	Engaging opening	>6% common abstract nouns	>4% it, this that, there	>4% be-verbs
Medicine	92	0	1	0	18	0	16
Evolutionary Biology	100	10	11	2	54	6	14
Computer Science	82	92	4	8	36	10	26
Higher Education	54	70	19	10	78	6	2
Psychology	84	58	14	18	60	30	16
Anthropology	88	78	31	28	30	12	12
Law	68	96	16	24	54	20	4
Philosophy	92	74	35	46	32	66	50
History	40	96	53	58	16	18	4
Literary Studies	96	92	77	52	20	14	0

Figure 2.1. Percentage of articles with various stylistic attributes in ten academic disciplines (n = five hundred; fifty articles per discipline). For more details, see the appendix.

that the science journals in my sample would all be highly prescriptive, tolerating very little variance in structure, titling, or
other points of style. This expectation proved true for medicine,
a field in which researchers tend to work in large teams and to
publish their findings using a standardized template. In evolutionary biology and computer science, however, I found considerably more expressive diversity. Ten percent of the evolutionary biologists in my sample opted for a unique or hybrid structure
in a field where the standard Introduction, Method, Results,
and Discussion (IMRAD) structure predominates; 8 percent of the
computer scientists use the IMRAD structure in a field where
hybrid structures predominate; and 11 percent of the evolutionary biologists and 8 percent of the computer scientists include at
least one "engaging" element in their titles, such as a quote, a
pun, or a question. These results were fairly evenly spread across
journals in both disciplines; that is, roughly 10 percent of the
articles *across the board* diverged from any given disciplinary
trend.

Another surprising finding was the predominance of first-
person pronouns in the sciences. The high percentages in medicine, evolutionary biology, and computer science (92, 100, and
82 percent, respectively) confound the commonly held assump-
tion that scientists shun the pronouns *I* and *we* in their research
writing. By contrast, only 54 percent of the higher education researchers in my data sample and only 40 percent of the historians
use first-person pronouns, a finding I discuss in further detail in
Chapter 4. Overall, I could identify no particularly strong correlation between pronoun usage and the number of authors per article; that is, single-authored articles are neither more nor less likely
than multiple-authored articles to contain first-person pronouns.
Nor did I find a single discipline in which first-person pronouns
are either universally required or universally banned. Even in literary studies, where first-person pronouns predominate, I counted
two *I*-less articles among the fifty surveyed.

Higher education researchers topped the table in their enthusiasm for nominalizations, those multisyllabic abstract nouns formed from verbs or adjectives—*obfuscation, viscosity, fortuitousness*—so beloved by academic writers. In 78 percent of the higher education articles, at least seven words out of every one hundred, and often many more, ended with one of seven common nominalizing suffixes *(-ion, -ism, -ty, -ment, -ness, -ance, -ence)*. By comparison, only 16 percent of the history articles contained a comparatively high density of nominalizations. Surprisingly, the philosophers in my sample—academics who specialize in abstraction—employ fewer nominalizations on average than their colleagues in evolutionary biology, computer science, higher education, psychology, or law. Philosophers do, however, turn to two other clusters of words associated with dense, passive prose—*is, are, was, were, be, been* and *it, this, that, there*—more than twice as often as academics in any of the other disciplines surveyed.

Psychology and anthropology proved the most challenging disciplines to characterize in terms of a "typical" style. Both are vast and varied social sciences with one foot each in the sciences and the humanities; the range and complexity of their subdisciplines cannot possibly be captured in a single snapshot. The five anthropology journals in my sample, for example, span a wide range of research activities—from the carbon dating of ancient jawbones to the development of new algorithms for explaining how social networks function—and differ starkly in their methodology, content, and style:

> Because the orientation of the femur could impact this measurement, the inferior curvature of the femoral necks of the specimens measured in this study were aligned with a photograph of a gorilla femur to standardize the superior-notch-depth measurement. [*Journal of Human Evolution*]
>
> It was shown in Dorogovtsev and Mendes (2000) that if the ageing function is a power law then the degree distribution has a phase transition from a power-law distribution, when the exponent of the

ageing function is less than one, to an exponential distribution, when the exponent is greater than one. [*Social Networks*]

It wasn't that I set out to test drive a sports car. Rather, on my way to work, I noticed rows of BMWs underneath a huge sign saying come and drive one, raise money for breast cancer. [*Cultural Anthropology*]

A similarly broad range of styles can be found in psychology, a discipline that ranges across all four quadrants of the "hard/soft," "applied/pure" typology first defined by Anthony Biglan.[9] Such disparities are, however, flattened in Figure 2.1, which represents average results across journals from ten different subdisciplines: applied psychology, biological psychology, clinical psychology, developmental psychology, educational psychology, experimental psychology, mathematical psychology, multidisciplinary psychology, psychoanalysis, and social psychology.

Figure 2.2 shows the average authorship, page length, and citation statistics for the ten disciplines surveyed. Most academics are aware that researchers in some disciplines publish short, multiauthored research reports while those in other fields favor long, single-authored articles. Nevertheless, the statistics for medicine (9.6 authors and 29 citations per 9 pages) versus law (1.4 authors and 152 citations per 43 pages) provide a striking visual contrast. For anyone who has ever sat on a multidisciplinary grant committee or promotion panel, Figure 2.2 offers a useful reminder that academics should never judge their colleagues' productivity or citational practices based solely on their own disciplinary norms.

Overall, my stylistic analysis confirms that most academic writers—except in highly prescriptive disciplines such as medicine—are shaped rather than ruled by convention. For nearly every disciplinary trend I identified, I noted stylistic exceptions: philosophers who opt *not* to employ first-person pronouns (8 percent); higher education researchers who opt *not* to begin every article with a bland, abstract sentence defining the significance of the research topic ("Academic writing is increas-

Discipline	# of authors	# of pages	# of citations
Medicine	9.6	9	29
Evolutionary Biology	3.8	21	54
Computer Science	2.7	27	27
Higher Education	1.8	24	48
Psychology	2.8	21	69
Anthropology	1.9	23	75
Law	1.4	43	152
Philosophy	1.1	24	50
History	1.1	26	78
Literary Studies	1	18	34

Figure 2.2. Average number of authors, page numbers, and citations or footnotes in articles from ten academic disciplines (n = five hundred; fifty articles per discipline). For more details, see the appendix.

ingly acknowledged as an important area of inquiry for higher education research") but instead capture their readers' attention with an opening anecdote, quotation, or question (10 percent). These statistics will, I hope, give courage to academics who want to write more engagingly but fear the consequences of violating disciplinary norms. A convention is not a compulsion; a trend is not a law. The signature research styles of our disciplines influence and define us, but they need not crush and confine us.

CHAPTER 3

A GUIDE TO THE STYLE GUIDES

Academic writing, like university teaching, is what sociologist Paul Trowler calls a "recurrent practice," one of the many routine tasks that most academics perform "habitually and in an unconsidered way," with little thought as to how or why things might be done differently: "It is simply taken for granted that this is what we do around here."[1] In recent years, with the advent of Preparing Future Faculty programs in the United States and faculty teaching certificates elsewhere, pedagogical training for academics has become something less of a novelty than it used to be. However, many early career academics still experience some version of the situation that I faced two decades ago when, freshly minted PhD in hand, I walked into my new department and was immediately presented with a list of the courses I had been assigned to teach in my first year. With no educational training and no explicitly developed pedagogical principles to call upon, I cobbled together courses that looked more or less exactly like the ones I had enrolled in as an undergraduate, and I delivered them in just the same way that they had been delivered to me, right down to the structure of my lectures and the wording of my exams. Occasionally I glanced around my department to see what my colleagues were up to; reassuringly, their practices mostly mirrored my own. Not until many years later did I discover that my university library was filled with row upon row of books devoted to topics such as student-centered learning and principles of course design—books that could have helped me become a more reflective, informed, and innovative teacher, had I only known that they existed.

The same is true with scholarly writing. For most academics, formal training on how to write "like a historian" or "like a biologist" begins and ends with the PhD, if it happens at all. For the remainder of our careers, we are left to rely on three main sources of guidance: our memories of what, if anything, our dissertation supervisors told us about good writing; occasional peer feedback on our work; and examples of recently published writing in the academic journals where we aspire to publish. All three tend to be forces for conservatism. Supervisors typically preach stylistic caution; they want their students to demonstrate mastery of disciplinary norms, not to push against disciplinary boundaries. Editors and referees, likewise, are often more intent on self-cloning than on genuine innovation or empowerment. Peer-reviewed publications, meanwhile, offer a range of stylistic models that are at best unadventurous and at worst downright damaging. Even the most prestigious international academic journals (as this book amply documents) may contain jargon-ridden, shoddily organized, sloppily argued, and syntactically imprecise prose. Academics who learn to write by imitation will almost inevitably pick up the same bad habits.

Of course, just as some academics become superb teachers despite their lack of formal training in higher education teaching, some researchers beat the odds and develop into superb writers. A few may even be fortunate enough to work with coauthors, mentors, or editors who push their writing in new directions rather than advising them to produce nothing but safe, "publishable" work. Only rarely, however, do advanced researchers turn to published writing guides as a means of developing and improving their writing. How do I know? Of the hundreds of academics I have talked to about their work as scholarly writers, only a few have mentioned books about writing as a significant source of their learning either during or beyond the PhD.

If academics read and heeded such books, what might the landscape of scholarly writing look like today? Curious to measure the distance between the advice offered in academic style guides and the realities of scholarly publishing, I engaged a research assistant to produce an annotated taxonomy of recently published books aimed at academic writers from across the disciplines. Her initial database search yielded more than five hundred entries; we winnowed this list down to one hundred writing guides, all published or in print in the years 2000–2010 and mostly targeted at advanced academics: that is, at graduate students and faculty. The list also included about a dozen generic style guides that one might expect to find on academics' bookshelves: acknowledged classics of the genre such as Strunk and White's *Elements of Style,* Gowers's *The Complete Plain Words,* Lanham's *Editing Prose,* and Williams's *Style: Lessons in Clarity and Grace.*

Of the one hundred books in our filtered sample, only 17 percent exclusively address university faculty, a significant statistic in its own right—apparently most publishers do not regard post-PhD academics as a viable market for writing guides. The vast majority of the guides (69 percent) target graduate students and/ or advanced undergraduates, while a few (8 percent) cater to academically trained professionals such as art and music critics, lawyers, and engineers. The books cover topics ranging from the basics of grammar and usage (*who* vs. *whom, effect* vs. *affect*) to the emotional and psychosocial aspects of writing (how to conquer writer's block, how to get along with one's dissertation advisor, how to establish a writing group). We focused specifically on what their authors had to say about the stylistic principles and techniques explored elsewhere in this book. Only two of these topics—clarity and structure—proved so universally compelling that they were discussed in more than 80 percent of the books examined. Several other key "elements of stylishness" such as

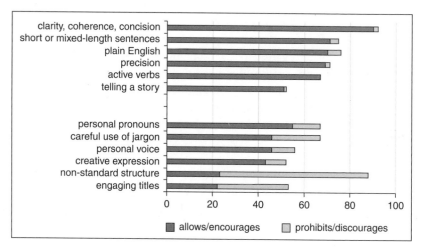

Figure 3.1. Percentage of advanced academic style guides that allow/encourage or prohibit/discourage twelve specific techniques associated with stylish writing (n = one hundred). For more details, see the appendix.

concrete language and opening hooks were mentioned in fewer than half the guides surveyed and therefore are not discussed here.

On six key points of style, the guides were virtually unanimous in their advice to academic authors (see Figure 3.1):

- *Clarity, Coherence, Concision:* Strive to produce sentences that are clear, coherent, and concise. (The "three Cs" are mentioned in some form in most of the style guides; only two guides out of one hundred explicitly argue *against* these values.)
- *Short or Mixed-Length Sentences:* Keep sentences short and simple, or vary your rhythm by alternating longer sentences with shorter ones.
- *Plain English*: Avoid ornate, pompous, Latinate, or waffly prose.

- *Precision:* Avoid vagueness and imprecision.
- *Active Verbs:* Avoid passive verb constructions or use them sparingly; active verbs should predominate.
- *Telling a Story:* Create a compelling narrative.

On six further questions, however, the guides offer inconsistent or conflicting recommendations:

- *Personal Pronouns:* Should academic authors use *I* and *we,* or not?
- *Careful Use of Jargon:* Should authors use specialist terminology when appropriate, or avoid disciplinary jargon altogether?
- *Personal Voice:* Should the writer be present in the writing (for example, via personal anecdotes, emotive responses, self-reflective commentary, and the development of a distinctive voice), or not?
- *Creative Expression:* Should academic authors use figurative language and other "creative" stylistic techniques, or should creative expression be avoided?
- *Nonstandard Structure:* Should articles and theses always follow a conventional structure, or are unique and experimental structures permitted?
- *Engaging Titles:* Should academic titles be playful and engaging, or should they be strictly informative?

From these mixed results, I draw two complementary conclusions. On the one hand, the guides' near unanimity on the first six items suggests that there are certain nonnegotiable principles that *all* academic writers would be well advised to follow. (One of the most damning findings of my research is that these principles are so often preached yet so seldom practiced.) On the other hand, the contradictory nature of the guides' advice on matters such as pronoun usage, structure, and titling reminds us just how complex and fraught the task of academic writing can be, especially for early career researchers who are still struggling to define a coherent academic identity.

Occasionally the writing guides' advice diverges along predictable disciplinary lines, as when 84 percent of the science guides but only 52 percent of the humanities guides recommend a standard structure for articles and theses. On most stylistic questions, however, the disciplines themselves are divided. For example, a majority of the guides (55 percent) advocate the use of personal pronouns, yet at least a few books in every disciplinary category (sciences, social sciences, humanities, and generic) caution against using *I* or *we*. Likewise, 43 percent of the guides commend creative forms of expression such as figurative or nonacademic language, but 9 percent (one or more from each major disciplinary category) warn *against* creativity in academic writing. How, then, are we to decide whose advice to follow?

To make matters even more confusing, the style guides themselves vary widely in academic register and style. About one-third (38 percent) employ an academic register characterized by complex syntax, sophisticated language, and abstract or theoretical ideas; nearly half (44 percent) maintain a generally formal but "plain English" tone; and the remainder (18 percent) introduce a more creative/colloquial style. Each of these three registers is fairly evenly distributed across the disciplines, suggesting that neither conventionality nor creativity holds a monopoly in any academic field. At the "creative/colloquial" end of the scale, authors use metaphor, wordplay, humor, personal anecdotes, experimental formal structures, and a raft of other stylish techniques to engage and inform their readers:

> A good first paragraph is all about striking the right note, or, to switch metaphors, giving your reader a firm handshake.[2]
>
> If you are more fastidious and you think things like, "I'll start writing just as soon as I've polished the underside of my Venetian blinds, alphabetized my CDs, and organised my rubber bands by size," steps must be taken.[3]
>
> Using theory is a tactic to cover the author's ass.[4]

At the "academic" end of the scale, by contrast, the writing in the style guides tends to sound much more, well, academic:

> The reason it is so difficult to make any progress in deciding how much support a premise *must* offer a conclusion in order for "[premise], therefore [conclusion]" to qualify as an argument is that it does not make a lot of sense to talk about what is a justification for what in the abstract.[5]
>
> Research nearly always requires the participation of many collaborators and an operational support structure, plus the professional institutions that enable individuals to acquire training (at a university for example) and to pursue research in a laboratory or in the field.[6]
>
> Such post hoc or retrospective theorizing reverses the directionality of the theory-research relationship.[7]

About three-quarters of the guides surveyed present their advice through indirect suggestion and examples rather than through direct imperatives such as *you must* or *you should*. Only a handful, however, explicitly foreground the principle of *choice*. Stephen Pyne documents the many stylistic options available to the confident stylist in the humanities, noting, for instance, that "colloquial language will grate against, even mock, a scholarly argument; so will exalted language in the service of the mundane. . . . Still for everything there is a time and place. A small dose of the vernacular can work like double washers on a machine bolt, allowing the parts to rotate without locking up."[8] Pat Francis superimposes art making with writing, incorporating creative materials into her own work—sketches, photos, collages, postcards, unusual uses of white space, diary entries, poetry, wordplay—and suggesting exercises designed to help researchers in arts disciplines flex their creative muscles.[9] Lynn Nygaard discusses epistemological issues such as objectivity, expressivism, personality, and transparency, bringing together science and humanities perspectives in a way that is rare in books aimed mainly at scientists.[10] Robert Goldbort offers a clear, readable account of science writing, including its history and public attitudes toward science writers; rather than demanding adherence to a rigid set of rules, Goldbort recognizes and encourages variety.[11] Angela Thody covers the basics of data collection, publication, and presentation, but also puts in a plug for alternative, even radically experimental, research modes.[12] Howard Becker dissects the writing culture of academia, corrects popular misconceptions about the writing process, catalogs common writing neuroses, and suggests practical strategies for negotiating the perils of publishing.[13] Finally, Stephen Brown analyzes the work of five leading marketing writers through the critical lenses of reader-response theory, Marxist literary theory, deconstruction, biopoetics, and psychoanalysis, respectively. Through his own novel approach to writing about academic writing, Brown actively resists what he calls the "identikit imperative" of most scholarly discourse.[14]

These authors make explicit what all of the writing guides in my sample, taken together, implicitly affirm through their many contradictions: academic writing is a process of making intelligent choices, not of following rigid rules. Yes, scholars in some fields have more freedom than others to make stylistic decisions that go against the disciplinary grain. Yes, convention remains a powerful force. Even in the most seemingly inflexible situations, however—for example, in journals where all research reports must conform to a rigid structural template—authors can still decide whether to write clear, concise, energetic sentences or opaque, complex, passive ones. Scientists can *choose* to use active verbs. Social scientists can *choose* to introduce a personal voice. Humanities scholars can *choose* to eschew disciplinary jargon. Informed choice is the stylish writer's best weapon against the numbing forces of conformity and inertia.

Cultural evolutionists Peter Richerson and Robert Boyd have observed that human beings tend to "imitate the common type" of any given cultural behavior: we do as others around us do, without stopping to wonder why. Occasionally, however, we can be persuaded to "imitate the successful" instead—for example, adapting our cooking style based on advice from a famous chef.

Cultures evolve, note Richerson and Boyd, only when "individuals modify their own behavior by some form of learning, and other people acquire their modified behavior by imitation."[15] For academic writers, the implications of this argument are clear: We can continue to "imitate the common type" of academic writing, endlessly replicating the status quo. We can "imitate the successful," adopting the stylistic strategies of eminent colleagues. Or we can undertake "forms of learning"—reading, reflection, experimentation—that will take our own work in new directions, so that we, in turn, can become the pathbreakers whose writing others will emulate.

In the chapters that follow, I discuss an array of techniques employed by scholars from across the disciplines to engage and inform their readers. Scattered throughout are callouts titled "Spotlight on Style," which gloss passages by exemplary writers whose work has been recommended to me by their discipline-based peers. In selecting from an initial list of more than one hundred suggested authors, I have sought to include examples from a wide range of academic fields and genres: from journal articles as well as from books, from highly specialized publications as well as from those aimed at a broader readership, and from conventional as well as deliberately creative academic prose. Readers will inevitably be able to name many other authors equally deserving of attention and emulation: colleagues whose writing they particularly admire, whether for its clarity or for its daring. I urge you to look to your own personal favorites for ideas and inspiration, as well as to the stylish authors profiled here. By "imitating the successful" and making their skills our own, we can collectively evolve the common type of academic writing into something truly worth reading.

THE ELEMENTS OF STYLISHNESS

CHAPTER 4

VOICE AND ECHO

Think of an academic writer whose work you particularly admire. Most likely you will choose someone whose words convey passion and commitment, whose writing engages you in a direct and visceral way; you feel as though this person is chatting with you over a cup of coffee, perhaps sketching diagrams on a napkin to illustrate a point, rather than lecturing to you in a monotonous voice from a computer printout or PowerPoint screen. Now think of an academic whose writing you find hard to digest, even if his or her ideas are perfectly sound. In nine cases out of ten, I'll wager, you will find the following:

- The author writes in an impersonal voice (the pronouns *I* and *we* might crop up occasionally, but could just as well be absent).
- The author makes no attempt to engage in a direct conversation with the reader (no humor, no asides, no engaging anecdotes, no *you*).
- The author writes paragraphs in which nearly every sentence either has an abstract noun as its subject ("this study," "the observation") or, thanks to grammatical sleight of hand, no named subject at all ("it can be seen," "the patients were examined").

Once upon a time, PhD students across the disciplines were taught that personality should never intrude upon scholarly writing. Apprentice scientists, social scientists, and even humanities scholars were warned that their research would not be taken seriously unless they reported on their work in a sort of human-free zone where *I* and *we* dared not speak their names. Some academics, forbidden to say *I*, resorted instead to the royal *we* ("in this paper, *we* [the solo author] will argue"), the inclusive *we* ("from these results, *we* [the author and readers] can surmise"), or awkward, third-person constructions ("*this writer* has argued elsewhere," "*the present researcher* has found"). Some took on a godlike persona, surveying the research landscape from on high and delivering subjective pronouncements in adverb-inflected language that cleverly disguised opinion as fact ("*cleverly* disguised opinion as fact"). Some let their research stand in as a kind of proxy for the absent *I* ("*this paper* will argue," "*this example* demonstrates"). And some twisted their sentences into passive verb constructions that hinted at but never acknowledged personal agency ("*it can be shown,*" "*the research was performed*").

These days, first-person pronouns are allowed in most academic disciplines: of the sixty-six peer-reviewed journals in my cross-disciplinary study, I found only one—a prominent history journal—that apparently forbids personal pronouns. Nevertheless, as the following examples from my data set demonstrate, academic writers still frequently employ the inclusive or royal *we:*

> In addition to questioning the class basis on which this long-accepted distinction rests, *we* need to create new histories of feminism that are no longer encumbered by problematic assumptions about women and putative class interests or by socialist politics of the past. [History]

They still couch their arguments in an impersonal yet authoritative style that represents opinion as fact:

Tax law is one of those areas that tends to be portrayed as discrete, dry and somewhat dull. The ECJ's recent direct tax jurisprudence *most definitely* does not fit that bill. [Law]

They still refer to themselves and their research teams in the third person:

The study investigators recruited the patients from March 2003 until April 2004 after a review of medical records and the completion of screening procedures to establish their eligibility for the trial. [Medicine]

They still ascribe agency to the research rather than to the researchers:

The concern of *this article* is language, and specifically the various projects of linguistic "purification" that were part of literary modernism in Britain. [Literary Studies]

And they still delight in contorting their sentences into passive or agentless constructions:

If, however, resemblance is identity, these features *can be explained* simply by appealing to the properties of identity. [Philosophy]

Nondeterminacy *is a fundamental notion* of computing with many important roles. [Computer Science]

Indeed, these last two phenomena—the "research as agent" sentence and the "agentless" sentence—occur so frequently in academic writing that both constructions can often be found cohabitating in a single paragraph:

Here *it is demonstrated* that the informativeness of a character can be quantified over a historical time scale. *This formulation* may play a role in resolving these controversies. [Evolutionary Biology]

If the authors of this article allowed themselves to speak as themselves—"Here we attempt to resolve some of those controversies by demonstrating"—their sentences would immediately become more energetic, more persuasive, and easier to understand.

NATHANIEL MERMIN

Your question was: Does this qualify as "strikingly different" enough to publish? I have never read anything like it, and I have read a lot on EPR [Einstein-Podolsky-Rosen Channels], though far from everything ever written. . . . After reading the paper I put it aside and spent the next week working hard on something totally unrelated. Every now and then I would introspect to see if some way of looking at the argument had germinated that reduced it to a triviality. None had. Last night I woke up at 3 a.m., fascinated and obsessed with it. Couldn't get back to sleep. That's my definition of "striking." So I say it's strikingly different and I say publish it.

In 1992, physicist Nathaniel Mermin was asked to review a discovery paper on "dense coding" for the journal *Physical Review Letters*. Although his words were originally intended for a private audience of one—namely, the journal's editor—the personal, passionate quality of Mermin's referee report suffuses nearly all his academic writing, from his titles to his chapter epigraphs:

- "The Amazing Many-colored Relativity Engine," *American Journal of Physics* [article title]
- "Copenhagen Computation: How I Learned to Stop Worrying and Love Bohr," *IBM Journal of Research and Development* [article title]
- "These 'bras' and 'kets'—they're just vectors!"—Newly enlightened computer scientist [chapter epigraph]

Mermin even manages to present mathematical formulas in a conversational mode tinged with humor:

- We begin with a silly formulation of ordinary non-quantum classical computing.
- While the operation X defined in (4) makes perfect sense for Obits (representing the logical NOT), the operation Z makes no sense at all.

His chatty style will not appeal to every scientist. All the same, we can see from these examples why Mermin, an expert communicator, has succeeded not only as a groundbreaking scientist but as the author of best-selling undergraduate textbooks and influential articles on the teaching of physics.

Social scientists often tell me that they have been trained to avoid *I* and *we,* even though the *APA Publication Manual,* the dominant style guide in the social sciences, has advocated the use of personal pronouns since 1974: "*We* means two or more authors or experimenters, including yourself. Use *I* when that is what you mean."[1] "So why aren't you allowed to write in the first person?" I ask my social science colleagues. "Well," they reply, "it's because we're supposed to sound objective, like scientists." Yet most scientists have long since abandoned the impersonal passive mode, a stance reflected in their most influential style manuals: the *ACS Style Guide* explicitly recommends using *I* or *we* when appropriate ("Use first person when it helps to keep your meaning clear and to express a purpose or a decision"), and the *AMA Manual* and the *CSE Manual* implicitly encourage first-person pronouns.[2] Thus we end up with the intriguing paradox that the evolutionary biologists in my data sample, who write mostly about plants and animals, use personal pronouns in every one of the fifty articles I surveyed (100 percent), while the higher education researchers, who write mostly about human beings, use *I* or *we* only about half the time (54 percent; see Figure 2.1 in Chapter 2).

An even more surprising anomaly occurs in the humanities, where only 40 percent of the historians in my data sample employ *I* or the personal *we,* in contrast to 92 percent of the philosophers and 98 percent of the literary scholars. Historians who avoid personal pronouns often insist that they do so as a means of maintaining an objective authorial stance. Yet of all the researchers in the ten disciplines I surveyed, the historians were the most clearly subjective—manipulative, even—in their use of language:

> This is admittedly a vast geographical and institutional canvas, and it is therefore necessary to focus on some issues to the exclusion of others.
>
> Fischer astutely responded that these polar approaches present false choices.

> Atlantic history has matured to the point where it needs to break out of the straitjacket imposed by the two models that have dominated interpretations of the historiography of the Americas.

These three examples were published in the *American Historical Review,* the only journal in my data sample that contains no first-person pronouns (aside from the collective *we*) in any of the articles I surveyed. The authors of these sentences never say *I;* however, they do pack their prose full of subjectively weighted nouns (*canvas, choices, straitjacket*), adjectives (*vast, necessary, polar, false, preset*), adverbs (*admittedly, astutely*), and verbs (*focus, matured, needs to break out, imposed, dominated, force, abandon*) designed to sway readers to a particular point of view. Compare the above sentences with the following extracts from *Isis,* a history of science journal in which first-person pronouns predominate:

> A few years ago I was stumped for several days by this question: Why is it that when we look in a mirror, left and right get reversed, but up and down do not?
>
> The scientific preeminence of the Paris museum in this period calls to mind that elegant phrase, "the power of place," that Janet Browne has used as the subtitle of the second volume of her biography of Charles Darwin. I think this is a wonderfully evocative phrase. With apologies to Janet if something is lost in geographical translation, I want to ask how the phrase could help us think about the Paris museum.

Writing with a frankly personal voice—"I was stumped," "I think this is a wonderfully evocative phrase"—these authors present themselves as fallible, emotive individuals. Their prose is not necessarily more elegant, eloquent, or well argued than that of their *I*-shunning colleagues. It is, however, more honest, making no attempt to camouflage opinion as historical truth.

So which mode is preferable? As with most questions of style, an author's decision whether or not to use personal pronouns remains very much a matter of personal taste. The "right"

JOHN HEILBRON

Perhaps Bohr's greatest strength was his ability to identify, and to exploit, failures in theory. His exercise of this ability amounted to a method. He would collect instances of failure, examine each minutely and retain those that seemed to him to embody the same flaw. He then invented a hypothesis to correct the flaw, keeping, however, the flawed theory to cover not only parts of experience where neither it nor the new hypothesis, with which it was in contradiction could account for phenomena. This juggling made for creative ambiguity as well as for confusion: Pushing the contradiction might disclose additional anomalies, and perhaps a better, more inclusive hypothesis. . . . To work in this way one needs not only creative genius, but also a strong stomach for ambiguity, uncertainty and contradiction.

Historian of science John Heilbron writes in the "impersonal historical" style favored by many historians, seldom if ever uttering the word *I*, yet nonetheless conveying a strong sense of authorial presence and persuasive power through his carefully selected verbs *(exploit)*, nouns *(genius)*, adjectives *(greatest)*, and adverbs *(minutely)*. Subtly rather than overtly, he nudges readers toward his own view—in this case, that the particular scientific genius of physicist Niels Bohr resided in his ability to embrace contradiction and failure.

Like all good science writers, Heilbron recognizes the importance of couching abstract ideas *(failure, theory, method, hypothesis, phenomena, anomalies, ambiguity, uncertainty, contradiction)* in concrete language. He describes instances of failure as quasi-physical entities that can be *collected, examined,* and *retained* like unusual rocks or rare biological specimens. Theories and hypotheses are *juggled,* contradictions are *pushed,* and anomalies are *disclosed.* Bohr needed a *strong stomach,* Heilbron tells us, to handle the kinds of "ambiguity, uncertainty and contradiction" (he might just as well have written "laboratory experiments involving maggots") that make other scientists queasy.

choice, then, is the one that the author has made consciously and carried through with consistency and craft. Some academics employ *I* or *we* to establish a deliberately familiar, conversational tone:

> Amid the silver jewelry as popular with foreigners as it is disdained by Yemeni women, who now favor gold, I was amused to find a doll that I immediately baptized "Chador Barbie." [Anthropology]

Some writers—particularly in science and social science disciplines where coauthored papers are the norm—take a more distanced stance, writing active, pronoun-driven sentences but making no attempt to build a direct connection with the reader:

> We extracted DNA from 3 different sample materials: blood, liver, and feces. . . . In addition, we used blood samples from 3 western gorillas from the Leipzig Zoo (Germany) and also a liver sample from a single deceased eastern gorilla (Gorilla beringei graueri) from the Zoo Antwerp (Belgium). [Evolutionary Biology]

Some authors, especially in the humanities, craft third-person prose that is nonetheless imbued with subjectivity and character:

> Settled by an extraordinarily literate people and long privileged by the American history establishment, colonial New England's every square inch has been seriously scrutinized. Or so the conventional wisdom has it. Consider this: Scholars have missed only 100,000 square miles, more or less, of terrain known intimately to seventeenth- and eighteenth-century villagers—the coastal ocean and its seafloor. The irony is superb, for the area seaward of the shore was the first part of the northwest Atlantic reconnoitered by Europeans. [History]

And some scholars write deliberately distanced, third-person prose that contains neither personal pronouns nor any vestige of a personal voice:

> The present research evaluates whether psychache mediates the influence of perfectionism on suicidal manifestations. [Psychology]

Each of these modes poses its own stylistic challenges. Academics who write highly subjective, first-person prose run the risk of sounding unprofessional and self-indulgent to their peers. Those who choose a mixed mode (personal pronouns with an impersonal voice or third-person pronouns with a subjective voice) must work through the potential inconsistencies of their personal-yet-distanced stance. Finally, those who favor third-person, impersonal prose need to ask themselves what they are trying to achieve by suppressing personal agency, especially given that so many of their academic colleagues, including research scientists, now employ first-person pronouns. "I write that way because I have to" turns out in most cases not to be a valid reason.

Coincidentally, the percentage of articles in my five hundred–article data sample that contain personal pronouns almost exactly matches the percentage of advanced academic writing guides in my one hundred–book sample that advocate personal pronoun usage (78 percent and 79 percent, respectively; see Figures 2.1 and 3.1 in Chapters 2 and 3). Nearly all of the peer-reviewed academic journals in my sample allow personal pronouns; however, I also found examples in every discipline of authors who avoid them and of writing guides that recommend against them. These seemingly contradictory statistics offer a message of empowerment and free will: pronoun usage is a matter of choice. Writers who feel uncomfortable using personal pronouns can produce strictly third-person prose if they prefer to, even in disciplines such as literature or philosophy, where first-person pronouns predominate. Meanwhile, those who have long avoided adopting a more personal voice out of habit, convention, or fear—perhaps because they were told by a teacher or supervisor long ago that personal pronouns sound "unprofessional" or "unacademic"—can relax and give *I* or *we* a whirl.

For many academic writers, permission to use personal pronouns comes as a tremendous relief. Referring to our actions in the first person ("*I* think," "*we* discovered") comes naturally to most humans; suppressing our own agency, by contrast, requires considerable syntactical effort and ingenuity. Most academics publish books and articles because we hope, on some level, to change our readers' minds: we want our colleagues to accept the validity of our data; to affirm the usefulness of our methodologies; to understand literary texts, historical events, philosophical problems, or legal issues in new ways. When we muzzle the personal voice, we risk subverting our whole purpose as researchers, which is to foster change by communicating new knowledge to our intended audience in the most effective and persuasive way possible.

Indeed, attention to audience is a hidden but essential ingredient of all stylish academic writing. One simple way to establish a bond with readers is to employ the second-person pronoun *you*, either directly or by means of imperative verbs, a mode particularly favored by philosophers and mathematical scientists:

> *Look* back at *your* parents' decision to bring *you* into the world. [Philosophy]
>
> *Consider* a large retail chain with multiple stores and warehouses, where products are ordered and shipped daily from the warehouses to replenish the inventory in the stores. [Computer Science]

However, academics can find many other ways of striking a conversational note and keeping an ear cocked for replies. You might visualize specific people looking over your shoulder as you write—the eminent colleague, the taxi driver, the curious high school student—and respond to their imagined questions. Peter Elbow urges a more direct approach: "You must walk up to readers and say, 'Let's go for a ride. You pedal, I'll steer.' "[3] Of course, no writer can expect to connect with *every* reader *every* time or to anticipate *every* possible response. All the same, the most engaging writers are almost invariably those who pay the closest attention to the real people—specialists and nonspecialists, colleagues and strangers—in whose ears their own words will echo.

RUTH BEHAR

Throughout most of the 20th century, in scholarly fields ranging from literary criticism to anthropology to law, the reigning paradigms have called for distance, objectivity, and abstraction. The worst sin has been to be "too personal." But if you're an African-American legal scholar writing about the history of contract law and you discover, as Patricia Williams recounts in her book *The Alchemy of Race and Rights . . . ,* the deed of sale of your own great-great-grandmother to a white lawyer, that bitter knowledge certainly gives "the facts" another twist of urgency and poignancy. It undercuts the notion of a contract as an abstract, impersonal legal document, challenging us to think about the universality of law and the pursuit of justice for all.

In an eloquent plea for academic writing that dares to say *I,* anthropologist Ruth Behar dares to say *you.* Rather than narrating legal scholar Patricia Williams's story using the third-person pronoun *she,* Behar puts us, squarely and perhaps uncomfortably, in Williams's own place: "If *you're* an African-American legal scholar . . . and *you* discover. . . ." Behar's tone is at once conversational and confrontational: she wants us on her side, but she also wants to rock the boat we're sitting in.

A passionate advocate of impassioned scholarly prose, Behar turns again to the second-person pronoun in her book *The Vulnerable Observer: Anthropology That Breaks Your Heart:*

When you write vulnerably, others respond vulnerably. . . . Call it sentimental, call it Victorian and nineteenth century, but I say that anthropology that doesn't break your heart just isn't worth doing anymore.

Challenging ethnographic conventions that privilege objectivity over human feeling, Behar joins a long line of anthropologists who have turned an incisive scholarly gaze on their own discipline. "To be able to write skillfully in a personal voice takes training and practice," Behar notes. Her own work offers living proof that it can be done.

THINGS TO TRY

- Choose a piece of your own writing and rate it according to the following chart. Circle one item per column (A, B, C, D):

	A (Pronouns)	B (Voice)	C (Perspective)	D (Register)
1.	*I* or *we*	Personal	Subjective	Informal
2.	No *I* or *we*	Impersonal	Objective	Formal

What happens if you change one or two of these variables? For example, if you usually write in a third-person, impersonal, objective, formal mode, introduce *I* or *we* and see how you feel about the results.

- Play around with *you*. For instance, you could start your opening paragraph with a direct exhortation to your reader ("Picture the following scene") or add a conversational aside ("You might wonder why"). Even if the second-person pronoun sounds too informal for your everyday writing, you can keep this trick up your sleeve for occasions when you especially need to establish a rapport with your audience, such as a conference presentation or a public lecture.

- Write down the names of at least *five real people* and tape the list to your computer screen. The list should include:

    - A top expert in your field (someone whom you would really like to impress)
    - A close colleague in your discipline (someone who would give you a fair and honest critique of your work)
    - An academic colleague from outside your discipline
    - An advanced undergraduate in your discipline
    - A nonacademic friend, relative, or neighbor.

Read your writing aloud and try to imagine each person's response to your words. Depending on discipline and context, you might not necessarily aspire to write in a way that all of these readers will understand all the time. Nevertheless, it can be an interesting exercise to think about how far each person is likely to get. For example, will the advanced undergraduate make it past the first paragraph of your article, your abstract, your title?

CHAPTER 5

SMART SENTENCING

A carefully crafted sentence welcomes its reader like a comfortable rocking chair, bears its reader across chasms like a suspension bridge, and helps its reader navigate tricky terrain like a well-hewn walking stick. A poorly crafted or uncrafted sentence, on the other hand, functions more like a shapeless log tossed into a river: it might or might not help you get to the other side, depending on how strong the current is and how hard you are willing to kick. And sometimes the reader of an academic text has to kick very hard indeed:

> These deconstructive and theorising inputs to the conversation are less about finding out how to better (i.e. more effectively) succumb to neo-liberal or economic rationalist discourses of effectiveness and completion, and more about critically exploring, for example, how those discourses may be operative and regulatory, what they make possible and impossible, and how they compete with other available discourses about the course and purpose of postgraduate research and supervision. [Higher Education]

So what's wrong with this sentence, as bumpy a log as one is likely to find floating in the waters of academe? For a start, the sentence has no clearly defined agent or action; its grammatical subject is an abstract noun *(inputs)* modified by a weak, spineless verb *(are)*. When we pose Richard Lanham's classic question, "Who's kicking whom?" we can deduce, with difficulty, that the sentence describes how academics in higher education use language.[1] Yet human beings remain mysteriously absent; the "neoliberal or economic rationalist discourses" that "compete with other available discourses" undertake their battle in a kind of agentless void. The many nouns scattered throughout the sentence *(inputs, conversation, discourses, effectiveness, completion, course, purpose, research, supervision)* are all relentlessly abstract, lumbered with equally abstract adjectives *(deconstructive, theorizing, neo-liberal, economic rationalist)* and strung together by prepositions *(to, about, to, of, about, for, with, about, of)* that send the reader's attention scudding off in one direction after the next. Thankfully, the sentence contains a few active verbs *(compete, find out, succumb, explore)*; however, the author neglects to tell us *who* will be doing the succumbing and exploring. Can such a waterlogged sentence be salvaged? Probably not. The author would be better off starting over again from scratch and building a stronger, leaner sentence with real people (postgraduate supervisors, discourse analysts) rather than "deconstructive and theorising inputs" at its core.

Academics identified by their peers as stylish writers for other reasons—their intelligence, humor, personal voice, or descriptive power—are invariably sticklers for well-crafted prose. Their sentences may vary in length, subject matter, and style; however, their writing is nearly always governed by three key principles that any writer can learn. First, they employ plenty of concrete nouns and vivid verbs, especially when discussing abstract concepts. Second, they keep nouns and verbs close together, so that readers can easily identify "who's kicking whom." Third, they avoid weighing down their sentences with extraneous words and phrases, or "clutter." Far from eschewing theoretical intricacy or syntactical nuance, stylish academic writers deploy these three core principles in the service of eloquent expression and complex ideas.

GILLIAN BEER

Most major scientific theories rebuff common sense. They call on evidence beyond the reach of our senses and overturn the observable world. They disturb assumed relationships and shift what has been substantial into metaphor. The earth now only *seems* immovable. Such major theories tax, affront, and exhilarate those who first encounter them, although in fifty years or so they will be taken for granted, part of the apparently common-sense set of beliefs which instructs us that the earth revolves around the sun whatever our eyes may suggest.

Academic writers often assume that abstract thought demands abstract language. Literary historian Gillian Beer lays that misconception firmly to rest. In the opening paragraph of *Darwin's Plots,* a study of the relationship between nineteenth-century science and literature, she describes how scientific theories *rebuff, call on, overturn, disturb,* and *shift* other forms of thinking; they *tax, affront,* and *exhilarate* the people who encounter them. Beer packs plenty of abstract nouns into this paragraph—*theories, common sense, evidence, reach, relationships, metaphor, beliefs*—but takes care to balance them with appeals to sensory experience: *senses, world, earth, sun, eyes.* Her writing helps us see how ideas and theories can take on energy and agency, a life of their own.

Beer's attention to style is evident also in the structure and pace of her prose. She starts off the paragraph with a short, compact sentence (seven words) followed by two slightly longer ones (fifteen and twelve words) and another very short one (six words). Then, just as we are getting used to her almost staccato rhythm, she tosses in a long, sinuous sentence (forty-seven words) that requires us to concentrate in quite a different way.

Only occasionally does Beer lose her touch and lapse into standard academese: "In this study I shall explore some of the ways in which evolutionary theory has been assimilated and resisted by novelists who, with the subtle enregisterment of narrative, have assayed its powers." Even the most stylish writers can sometimes have a bad sentence day.

Concrete language is arguably the single most valuable tool in the stylish writer's toolbox. When readers encounter a sentence composed largely of concrete nouns, they can immediately visualize its objects, actions, and relationships, as when philosopher Kwame Anthony Appiah illuminates the universality of the human condition by describing a time-traveling baby:

> If a normal baby girl born forty thousand years ago were kidnapped by a time traveler and raised in a normal family in New York, she would be ready for college in eighteen years. She would learn English (along with—who knows?—Spanish or Chinese), understand trigonometry, follow baseball and pop music; she would probably want a pierced tongue and a couple of tattoos.[2]

A sentence composed mostly of abstract nouns, by contrast, offers us nothing tangible to hang on to, no person or thing that we can mentally situate in physical space:

> Replicating the post-Mendel application of Lamarck's apparently superseded scientific theory by non-empirical social scientists, Vernon Lee's fervent and intellectually original use of scientific paradigms across different fields in order to further a specific literary and creative heuristic offers an exemplary narrative trace, replete with hybridized methodologies and the rhetorical deployment of scientific language in non-scientific discourses. [Literary Studies]

This sentence suffers from other ailments as well, including a paralyzing glut of adjectives and adverbs *(fervent, intellectually original, scientific, different, specific, literary, creative, exemplary, hybridized, rhetorical, scientific, non-scientific)* and a shocking case of jargonitis *(paradigms, heuristic, trace, hybridized)*. But even with its adjectives eliminated and its vocabulary toned down, so many abstract nouns compete here for the reader's attention—*application, theory, use, paradigms, fields, heuristic, trace, methodologies, deployment, language, discourses*—that we lose sight of the sentence's fundamental message: Vernon Lee's writing deserves scholarly attention because she applied scientific thinking to her literary endeavors in original and interesting ways.

Stylish writers sometimes bring intangible concepts to life by pairing abstract nouns with animating verbs:

> Substantive differences also lurk in this confusion.[3]
>> Play, like sleep and dreaming, puzzles and fascinates biologists.[4]

In these lively sentences by philosopher Daniel Dennett and literary scholar Brian Boyd, respectively, *differences* and *play* function almost like living characters; they have physical presence *(lurk)* and affective agency *(puzzles* and *fascinates)*. Many academics, however, give little thought to their verbs, favoring forms of *be (is, am, are, was, were, been)* and predictable scholarly verbs such as *analyze, show, examine,* and *consider:*

> Although standard statistical methods *are* available for incorporating measurement error and other sources of variation, they are not commonly applied, and they have rarely been *considered* in the context of phylogenetic statistics in which trait values are *correlated* among related species. [Evolutionary Biology]

The authors of this evolutionary biology article, for example, have combined three abstract verbs *(apply, consider, correlate)* with a series of *be* verbs *(are, are, been, are)* to produce a passively phrased sentence in which we never actually discover who is doing (or failing to do) all that applying, considering, and correlating. Compare their lackluster effort with another article from the same journal:

> Insects suck, chew, parasitize, bore, store, and even cultivate their foods to a highly sophisticated degree of specialization. [Evolutionary Biology]

These authors hook us in straightaway with a concrete noun *(insects)* and a series of equally concrete verbs *(suck, chew, parasitize, bore, store, cultivate)* that leave us in absolutely no doubt as to "who's kicking whom."

Abstract nouns weigh down the prose of researchers in nearly every academic discipline, from medicine to literary theory. All scholarly endeavor involves abstract thinking, of course, which we naturally express via abstract language. The problems occur when we allow abstract nouns to take over and multiply, even in sentences that describe the actions and attributes of concrete entities such as people, places, and things:

> According to de Man, the robustness of this incoherence, the failure of the sublime to secure an exit from skepticism through philosophical argument, indicates that Kant's analysis relies on rhetorical sleight of hand. [Literary Studies]
>
> The original objective of the sanitation project, known as Bahia Azul or Blue Bay, was the control of marine pollution, which was largely caused by the discharge of domestic waste water. [Medicine]

As readers, we have to struggle unacceptably hard to locate the agents and actions in these sentences, even though each contains two proper nouns *(de Man, Kant; Bahia Azul, Blue Bay)* and one concrete noun *(hand, water)*. In both sentences, the grammatical subject is an abstract noun that sits miles away from its accompanying verb: "*the objective* [eleven words] *was*"; "*the robustness* [seventeen words] *indicates.*" What are the authors really trying to say here? "*We designed* the sanitation project to control marine pollution"; "*De Man argues* that *Kant relies* on rhetorical sleight of hand."

Clutter, the sworn enemy of the stylish academic writer, denotes all those extraneous words and phrases that get in the way of a sentence's meaning, whether by driving nouns and verbs apart or by tripping up readers in other ways. Among the most persistent contributors to clutter are *prepositions*: little linking words such as *of, by, to,* and *through.* In a well-calibrated sentence, prepositions supply energy and directional thrust:

> The backbone of this system was a chain of command which ran from the monarch; to the department of government which drafted the instructions which guided the voyage, selected the ship and

ANNE SALMOND

When the *Dolphin* arrived at Tahiti, the island was "discovered" and the islanders entered European history. Equally, however, the Europeans entered Tahitian history, tangling these histories together. Wallis was searching for Terra Australis Incognita, hoping to inscribe its coastlines on the maps of the world, while the Tahitians thought that the *Dolphin* was a floating island, or perhaps a craft from Te Po, the realm of ancestors.

In an article whose very title expresses equipoise—"Their Body Is Different, Our Body Is Different: European and Tahitian Navigators in the 18th Century"—anthropologist Anne Salmond moves gracefully back and forth between European and Tahitian perspectives on the European "discovery" of Tahiti. Through carefully balanced parallel sentences, she grants equal agency to both parties—"the islanders entered," "the Europeans entered"—and equal weight to their beliefs and perceptions: "Wallis was searching," "the Tahitians thought."

Salmond's sentences are concise, verb driven, and chock-full of concrete detail:

In unfamiliar waters a skilled navigator could identify and name new swells by studying the sea hour after hour, and the sequence of stars, the wind and current patterns and numerous other items of navigational information were memorized for the return voyage. During such expeditions the navigator slept as little as possible, ceaselessly scanning the sea and the night sky and keeping watch for land clouds and homing birds. It was said that you could always recognize a star navigator by his blood-shot eyes.

In simple, economical language, she conveys the extraordinary complexity of the star navigator's task, which involved apprehending numerous physical details *(waters, swells, sea, sequence of stars, wind, current patterns, night sky, land clouds, homing birds)* and interpreting them by calling upon a range of intellectual skills *(identify, name, study, memorize, scan)*. Salmond's account of European and Polynesian navigational expertise is evenhanded yet deeply felt, fueled by a self-professed ambition to "do justice to the complex, many-sided dynamics of these engagements."

appointed its crews; to the captain, who had supreme command of the ship, within his orders and a strict set of naval conventions; to the officers and the petty officers; and down to the ordinary sailors.[5]

All too often, however, authors use prepositions to string together long sequences of abstract nouns:

> This conceptual distinction between anticipatory and consummatory pleasure is supported by evidence from functional magnetic resonance imaging studies of healthy individuals, which has differentiated the relative role of brain regions involved in anticipation of a future reward (nucleus accumbens) in contrast with consumption of rewards (prefrontal cortex). [Psychology]

In the first of these two extracts, by anthropologist Anne Salmond, prepositions clarify relationships; in the second, they obscure them, leaving the reader to extract the author's meaning (who's kicking whom?) from a tangled skein of ideas.

Adjectives and *adverbs* add color and zest to stylish scholarly prose. Like prepositions, however, they can also contribute to clutter:

> In the first part of this essay, I reexamine the trajectory of thinking from Lamarck to Mendel and beyond in the revivifying light of an additional premise: that scientific paradigms were used in creative ways by ostensibly empirical evolutionary scientists in the absence of clinching verifiable evidence—a process that would reach its apogee with the exposure of Paul Kammerer's Lamarckian toad hoax. [Literary Studies]

The author of this passage has flung one descriptive adjective after another *(revivifying, additional, scientific, creative, empirical, evolutionary, clinching, verifiable, Lamarckian)* into an already long and complex sentence that raises more questions than it answers. Can a light be *revivifying* (that is, capable of bringing dead things to life)? Can a trajectory be *revivified* (was the trajectory ever dead in the first place)? Did the creative misappropriation of scientific paradigms reach its apogee with the exposure of Kammerer's toad hoax, or with the toad hoax itself? Does the word *evidence*—signifying something that helps us form a conclusion or judgment—really require the addition of both *clinching* and *verifiable* to make its meaning apparent? The harder we pull on the interlocking threads of this sentence, the more clearly we see that it exhibits all of the other familiar problems already outlined in this chapter: predictable academic verbs *(reexamine, use, reach)*; a glut of abstract nouns *(trajectory, thinking, premise, paradigms, ways, absence, evidence, process, apogee, exposure, hoax)*; and long sequences of prepositional phrases ("the trajectory *of* thinking *from* Lamarck *to* Mendel and *beyond in* the revivifying light *of* an additional premise") that make us lose sight of its main idea.

Other contributors to clutter include *it, this, that,* and *there.* These four eminently useful little words have a place in every stylish writer's repertoire. Used carelessly or excessively, however, they can muddy rather than clarify meaning:

> It is now generally understood that constraints play an important role in commonsense moral thinking and generally accepted that they cannot be accommodated by ordinary, traditional consequentialism. [Philosophy]

The author of this article uses *it* to make sweeping, passively phrased claims about other people's (or at least other philosophers') alleged thought and beliefs: "*It* is now generally understood that" and "*It* is now generally accepted that." In the very next sentence, the author stirs *this* into the mix:

> Some have seen this as the most conclusive evidence that consequentialism is hopelessly wrong, while others have seen it as the most conclusive evidence that moral common sense is hopelessly paradoxical.

Some *who* have seen this *what*? A diligent reader can deduce that *this* and *it* serve as shorthand for something like "the fact that traditional consequentialism cannot accommodate the constraints involved in commonsense moral thinking." But why

JAMES WEBSTER

The minor mode itself has a different tinta in each: wild and untamed in the Farewell, densely passionate in the quartet, grace in the trio. The three endings alone—ethereal, tragic, melancholy—would suffice to make the point. It bears repeating: Haydn never repeats himself.

Historian of music James Webster turns musical movements into dramatic narratives and symphonies into stories. In his classic full-length study of Haydn's "Farewell" Symphony, he lets his language soar to lyrical levels as he summons one adjective after another—*wild, untamed, passionate, ethereal, tragic, melancholy*—to illustrate the emotive power of Haydn's minor mode. Elsewhere his vocabulary becomes highly technical. Yet even when addressing a specialist audience, he continues to call on perfectly chosen adjectives *(deceptive, quickly)* and lively verbs *(leads, bursts, harmonized)* to convey drama and action:

The deceptive cadence in m. 182 leads quickly to vii [4 over 3] (yet another dominant; note the high e1 in the bass) and a fermata; then the Presto bursts in with the headmotive d, harmonized by a forte, root-position V-I cadence—the first and only such conjunction in the movement.

Alert to the power of a good story, Webster often frames his musical analyses with tales of human escapades and foibles:

Every music-lover knows the story of Haydn's "Farewell" Symphony. Each year, the Esterházy court spent the warm season at Prince Nicolaus's new and splendid, but remote, summer castle "Esterháza."

If Schubert was homosexual, as Maynard Solomon suggests in his now-famous essay, what difference does it make for his music?

Describing Haydn's sojourn at Esterházy, he lays on a series of adjectives *(warm, new, splendid, remote)*; addressing Schubert's alleged homosexuality, he poses a blunt question. Exquisitely attentive to subtleties of musical style, Webster varies his own style to fit his purpose.

should we have to work so hard? Isn't it the author's job, not ours, to make the sentence's meaning clear?

There is a mostly unremarkable word that contributes to clutter by consorting with *it, this, that, be* verbs, and other bad company:

> If the nomocentric principle is correct, then there are as many true backward counterfactual conditionals as there are forward counterfactual conditionals and, therefore, the thesis that an asymmetry of counterfactual dependence characterizes our world would turn out to be false. [Philosophy]

And what's wrong with *that?* When used as a determiner ("*that* girl," "*that* hat"), nothing at all. However, in its grammatical function as a relative pronoun, *that* often encourages writers to overload their sentences with subordinate clauses, driving nouns and verbs apart in the process:

> In a series of important papers, John Broome has argued that the only sense of "should" at work here is the one that we use in saying what there is most reason, or decisive reason, to do and that the apparent contradiction in the example is removed when we make appropriate distinctions of scope. [Philosophy]

Here, *that* occurs three times in a single sentence, twice as part of a parallel construction ("John Broome has argued *that* . . . and *that*") and once as part of an intervening clause ("the one *that* we use"). An attentive stylist would reword or eliminate the latter, which gets in the way of the parallel *that* clauses on either side.

Note that all of the above examples were drawn from recent articles in philosophy journals. Philosophers are by no means the only academic writers whose sentences are awash in *it, this, that,* and *there.* On average, however, they use these four words much more frequently than academics in other disciplines—a statistic that helps to explain why many nonphilosophers find philosophical prose wordy, dense, and difficult to read. In my data sample of peer-reviewed publications from ten different disciplines, the percentage of articles in which *it, this, that,* and *there* constitute forty or more of the first thousand words, excluding quotations and citations, ranged from 0 percent in medicine to 30 percent in psychology. For philosophy, the figure was 65 percent, more than double the density in the next-highest discipline (see Figure 2.1 in Chapter 2). So is there something special about philosophical discourse that makes it imperative for philosophers to write in this wooden, long-winded way? In a study of multidisciplinary peer review panels in the United States, sociologist Michèle Lamont found that philosophers tend to regard their own field as "uniquely demanding," whereas their colleagues from other disciplines commented that "philosophers live in a world apart from other humanists" and "what philosophers do is irrelevant, sterile, and self-indulgent."[6] Philosophers who are content to live and write in "a world apart" need not be concerned by my survey statistics, which merely reaffirm their uniqueness. However, those who aspire to communicate with nonspecialists—students, colleagues, the general public, and the academics on those all-important multidisciplinary review panels that can make or break an academic career—might start by addressing their addiction to *it, this, that,* and *there.*

Any of the "smart sentencing" principles outlined in this chapter can, of course, be temporarily suspended for rhetorical effect. Obituary writers understand the dramatic value of widely separating a subject and its accompanying verb:

> J. D. Salinger, who was thought at one time to be the most important American writer to emerge since World War II but who then turned his back on success and adulation, becoming the Garbo of letters, famous for not wanting to be famous, died on Wednesday at his home in Cornish, N.H., where he had lived in seclusion for more than 50 years.[7]

Stylish academic writers, likewise, often play around with language: they vary their vocabulary, mix up their syntax, and veer back and forth between short sentences and long. Passive verb constructions may even be allowed into their prose from time to time. They follow no set formula or rule book; but nor do they throw grammar and coherence to the wind. Whatever their stylistic choices, they always make us feel that every word counts.

THINGS TO TRY

- For a playful insight into what ails a sagging paragraph, go to the Writer's Diet Web site (http://www.writersdiet.com) and paste a sample of your writing (one thousand words maximum) into the online WritersDiet test, a free diagnostic tool designed to tell you whether your sentences are "flabby or fit."[8] The test automatically highlights words in five grammatical categories commonly associated with stodgy academic prose—*be* verbs, nominalizations, prepositions, adjectives/adverbs, and *it, this, that, there*—and indicates whether those words occur in unusually high quantities. By the time you have tested three or four samples of your writing, you will have become aware of your signature usage patterns—for example, a predilection for abstraction (translation: too many spongy abstract nouns) or a tendency to begin every sentence with *this*.

- Replace at least a few *be* verbs in every paragraph with active, unusual verbs. A sentence powered by vivid verbs *(sway, shun, masquerade)* will speak to your readers more effectively than one that contains only forms of *be* ("The experiment *was*") and predictable academic verbs ("This proposition *shows*").

- Identify all your *passive verb constructions,* which are usually signaled by the presence of a *be* verb plus a past-tense verb *(are signaled, can be shown, is affected).* Passive constructions can be employed by stylish writers for a number of reasons; in the first part of this sentence, for example, the phrase "Passive constructions can be employed by stylish writers" places *passive constructions* front and center, whereas an actively worded phrase such as "Stylish writers employ passive constructions" would have put more weight on the author's role. A few passive phrases can provide welcome syntactical variety. Too many passive constructions in one paragraph, however, will add up to lifeless, agentless prose.

- If you are like most academic writers, your writing sample probably contains a high percentage of *nominalizations,* which are abstract nouns formed from verbs or adjectives through the addition of a suffix such as *-ance, -ence, -ity, -ness, -ion, -ment,* or *-ism.* To reduce their stultifying effect:

  - Make sure that at least one sentence per paragraph includes a concrete noun or a human entity as its subject, immediately followed by an active verb ("Merleau-Ponty argues," "Students believe," "International banks compete").
  - Animate abstract nouns with active verbs ("Nominalizations *suck* the energy out of your sentences").
  - Cut down on prepositional phrases, especially where they string together long sequences of abstract nouns ("the representation *of* female desire *in* an era characterized *by* the objectification *of* personal experience"). When in doubt, limit the number of prepositional phrases to no more than three in a row.
  - Where possible, explain abstract concepts using concrete examples.

- Measure the distance between nouns and their accompanying verbs. When agent and action become separated by more than about a dozen words, readers quickly lose the plot. (Example: "The *knowledge* that criminalization of marijuana use can lead to a wide variety of other social ills, including an increased risk of addiction to more dangerous and expensive drugs such as heroine and cocaine, *has not prevented* lawmakers. . . .") Ideally, a noun and its accompanying verb should pack a quick, one-two punch: "Lawmakers know . . ."

- If your WritersDiet test results reveal a weakness for adjectives and adverbs, ask yourself whether you really need them all. Can you supply the same descriptive energy using concrete nouns and lively verbs?
- Is your prose overly dependent on *it, this, that,* and *there?* If so, try adhering to the following principles next time you write something new:

  - Use *this* only when accompanied by a modifying noun ("This *argument* shows" rather than merely "*This* shows"). Writers often slip *this* into their sentences to avoid stating their ideas clearly ("Some have seen *this* as conclusive evidence that . . .").
  - Use *it* only when its referent—that is, the noun *it* refers to—is crystal clear. For example, in the sentence "The woman threw the lamp through the window and broke *it,*" what did the woman break, the lamp or the window?
  - Avoid using *that* more than once in a single sentence or about three times per paragraph, except in a parallel construction or for stylistic effect. Sentences that rely on subordinate clauses that in turn contain other clauses that introduce new ideas that distract from the main argument that the author is trying to make . . . well, you get the idea.
  - Use *there* sparingly. There is no reason why you should not employ *there* every now and then. But wherever *there* is, weak words such as *this, that, it,* and *is* tend to congregate nearby. Example: "*There are* a number of studies *that* show *that this is* a bad idea because *it* . . ."

Do you find all of this editorial polishing and tweaking laborious and slow? Remember, stylish academic writers spend time and energy on their sentences so their readers won't have to!

CHAPTER 6

TEMPTING TITLES

Like a hat on a head or the front door to a house, the title of an academic article offers a powerful first impression. Is the title dry, technical, straightforward? Most likely, the author's main goal is to transmit research data as efficiently as possible. Does the title contain opaque disciplinary jargon? Perhaps the author unconsciously hopes to impress us, whether by appealing to a shared expertise ("You and I are members of an exclusive club") or by reminding us of our ignorance ("If you can't even understand my title, don't bother reading any further"). Is the title amusing, intriguing, provocative? Here is an author who is working hard to catch our gaze, engage our interest, and draw us in. In many disciplines, however, such a move goes against the academic grain and even contains a significant element of risk: a "catchy" title might well be regarded by colleagues as frivolous and unscholarly.

Several years ago, I attended a higher education research conference at which a presentation titled "Evaluating the E-learning Guidelines Implementation Project: Formative and Process Evaluations" was offered at the same time as one called "'Throwing a Sheep' at Marshall McLuhan." Guess which session drew the bigger audience? "Throwing a sheep" is a method of getting someone's attention on the popular social-networking Web site Facebook; Marshall McLuhan is the educator and media theorist who famously coined the phrases "global village" and "the medium is the message." A delegate at a conference on higher education research could thus reasonably surmise that a presentation containing the phrases "throwing a sheep" and "Marshall McLuhan" would explore the role of social-networking Web sites in university teaching and learning. That expectation was confirmed in the conference program, in which a lively abstract spelled out the main argument of the presentation, gave further hints of the author's penchant for quoting colorful student argot ("pinch, moon, drop kick, spank, poke, b#%*! slap, drunk dial"), and asked a series of questions aimed at the expected audience of educators and educational theorists.[1]

The "throwing a sheep" example illustrates the crucial function of the *paratext* in academic titling. Described by literary theorist Gérard Genette as a zone of transition and transaction between "text and non-text," a paratext consists of all the extratextual matter that accompanies and packages a text: for example, the cover of a book, the publisher's blurb, the author's name, the preface, the dedication, the typography, and the illustrations.[2] Titles belong both to text and paratext; they shape our reading of the text yet are also inflected by other paratextual elements. In the case of the "throwing a sheep" talk, the inclusion of a detailed abstract in the conference program freed up the presenter to concoct a playful but enigmatic title, secure in the knowledge that further information about the session could easily be accessed elsewhere. Moreover, the title of the conference—"Tertiary Education Research"—supplied the attendees with additional paratextual clues. Delegates at a higher education research conference would naturally expect all the presentations to address aspects of higher education research; thus, there was no need for the presenter to add a ponderous explanatory subtitle containing the words "higher education research."

Supplementing the role of the paratext is a title's *subtext,* which consists of messages from the author that are not stated directly in words but can be inferred by an attentive reader. The subtext of "'Throwing a Sheep' at Marshall McLuhan" might read something like this: "I am the kind of academic who likes to entertain and engage an audience. This session will be playful, not plodding. You can expect me to use lots of concrete examples and visual illustrations." Whether the presentation will live up to these expectations is, of course, another matter—and one that stylish authors need to take into consideration as part of the titling process. If you run a spartan hotel, you probably should not advertise it with an ornate front door.

Attention to paratext and subtext can help academic writers make more thoughtful—and in some cases more daring—decisions about their titles. A scientist presenting new research findings to specialist colleagues might choose a serious, functional title studded with specialist terminology (subtext: "You can trust my results because my research has been conducted according to the highest scientific standards"). However, when invited to participate in a university lecture series aimed at members of the general public, the same scientist faces a wider range of choices—and a correspondingly greater variety of possible subtexts. The title could be purely informational, describing the topic of the lecture in clear and simple terms (subtext: "My lecture will be informative and lucid, but possibly rather dull"). It could be stuffed full of scientific jargon (subtext: "You will have to work very hard to understand me"). It could be playful ("I want to entertain you"), alliterative ("My talk, like my title, will be carefully crafted"), and/or provocative ("I want to make you think"). Every one of these choices carries both benefits and risks; the same subtext that attracts one reader could easily turn another off. Most undergraduates learn to negotiate this stylistic dilemma fairly quickly: the safest title is the one their teacher will approve of. Similarly, graduate students writing a thesis or dissertation know they need to satisfy only a few readers (subtext: "I am one of you now. I know the rules of the game; please admit me to your disciplinary fraternity"). As an academic writer's potential audience expands, however, so does the range of choices.

OLIVER SACKS

For one of my deeply parkinsonian post-encephalitic patients, Frances D., music was as powerful as any drug. One minute I would see her compressed, clenched and blocked, or else jerking, ticking and jabbering—like a sort of human time bomb. The next minute, if we played music for her, all of these explosive-obstructive phenomena would disappear, replaced by a blissful ease and flow of movement, as Mrs. D., suddenly freed of her automatisms, would smilingly "conduct" the music, or rise and dance to it. But it was necessary—for her—that the music be legato; for staccato, percussive music might have a bizarre countereffect, causing her to jump and jerk helplessly with the beat, like a mechanical doll or marionette.

Writing in the journal *Brain* about the druglike power of music to calm or agitate the brain, neurologist Oliver Sacks conveys a clinician's verbal precision ("deeply parkinsonian post-encephalitic," "explosive-obstructive"), a storyteller's attention to character ("Mrs. D. . . . would smilingly 'conduct' the music"), a poet's love of metaphor ("human time bomb," "like a mechanical doll or marionette"), and a musician's sensitivity to rhythm and sound ("jerking, ticking and jabbering," "a blissful ease and flow"). Lauded by the *New York Times* as "a kind of poet laureate of contemporary medicine," Sacks has published numerous cleverly titled books about his clinical work with patients:

- *Awakenings*
- *The Man Who Mistook His Wife for a Hat and Other Clinical Tales*
- *An Anthropologist on Mars: Seven Paradoxical Tales*
- *Musicophilia: Tales of Music and the Brain*
- *The Island of the Colorblind*
- *A Leg to Stand On*
- *Uncle Tungsten: Memories of a Chemical Boyhood*

Richly varied rather than formulaic, each of these titles incorporates at least one of the following elements associated with engaging writing: a concrete image *(hat, colorblind, leg)*; a surprising juxtaposition *(wife/hat, anthropologist/Mars, chemical boyhood)*; a pun or wordplay (awakenings, musicophilia); and a reference to storytelling *(tales, memories)*.

Among the many decisions faced by authors composing an academic title, the most basic choice is whether to *engage* the reader, *inform* the reader, or do both at once. Deliberately engaging titles are standard fare in the world of book publishing, particularly on that slippery slope where academic discourse meets the educated reading public. For example, the best-selling popular science books by evolutionary biologist Richard Dawkins typically sport titles that contain just a few carefully chosen words:

- *The Selfish Gene* (1976)
- *The Blind Watchmaker* (1986)
- *Climbing Mount Improbable* (1996)[3]

But lest we be tempted to assume that catchy titles are a luxury afforded only to the famous few—those rare academics who have descended from the ivory tower into the lucrative world of trade publishing—it is instructive to note that Dawkins already favored them long before he started writing for the general public. An early research letter, published in 1969 in *Science,* bore the beautifully catchy *and* descriptive title "Bees Are Easily Distracted."[4] It seems that Dawkins already understood early in his career what many academics never learn: it is possible to write compelling titles and to be a respected researcher at the same time.

Another striking example of an engaging *and* informative academic title comes from a major medical study published in the United Kingdom in 2006: "Why Children Die: A Pilot Study."[5] Significantly, the authors of this study were not writing only for other medical researchers like themselves; they intended their report to be accessible to a far wider range of readers, including health practitioners, social workers, politicians, and the general public. In fact, two different versions of the report were made available: a 124-page version aimed at adults and a 14-page summary for children and young people. The title, which is the same for both versions, raises some provocative questions. Why *do* children die, how many, and under what circumstances? What steps can be taken to improve the child mortality rate in the United Kingdom? What work is already being done, and what future research is planned as a result of the pilot study? Imagine the same report in the hands of a medical academic: "Methodological and Practical Considerations in the Conduct of a Confidential National Enquiry on Child Mortality: A Feasibility Study." Rather than bludgeoning us with lots of technical language or anesthetizing us with abstract jargon, the title "Why Children Die" invites us to turn the page and start reading.

As James Hartley and other scholars have noted, the simplest way to generate an "engaging *and* informative" title is to join together two disparate phrases (one catchy, the other descriptive) using a colon, semicolon, or question mark.[6] Literary scholars are particularly fond of the "engaging: informative" technique:

- "The First Strawberries in India: Cultural Portability in Victorian Greater Britain"
- "#$%^&*!?: Modernism and Dirty Words"
- "The Coachman's Bare Rump: An Eighteenth-Century French Cover-Up"

This method is also popular with historians:

- "'Every Boy and Girl a Scientist': Instruments for Children in Interwar Britain"
- "Women on Top: The Love Magic of the Indian Witches of New Mexico"

Variations on the "engaging: informative" structure can be found in nearly every academic discipline. Only in the humanities, however, is there a strong correlation between the percentage of "engaging and informative" titles and the overall rate of colon usage. When I rated the titles of the one thousand academic articles in my data sample as "engaging," "informative," or both, I found that only 22 percent, mostly from the humanities, could be classified as "both engaging and informative," yet 48 percent overall contain colons.[7]

BOB ALTEMEYER

The world's a stage for billions of wonderfully unique people. But what would it be like if everyone had similar levels of some personality trait? If all the actors scored relatively high in right-wing authoritarianism, what kind of future would unfold?

In the opening paragraph of an article with the catchy *and* descriptive title "What Happens When Authoritarians Inherit the Earth? A Simulation," psychologist Bob Altemeyer invites us to imagine an alternative universe in which the world is populated entirely by people attracted to right-wing authoritarianism ("high RWAs"). Such people, he explains, have proven

relatively submissive to government injustices, unsupportive of civil liberties and the Bill of Rights, . . . mean-spirited, ready to join government "posses" to run down almost everyone (including themselves), happy with traditional sex roles, strongly influenced by group norms, highly religious (especially in a fundamentalist way), and politically conservative (from the grass roots up to the pros, say studies of over 1,500 elected lawmakers).

In the next section, titled "The Plot Thickens: High SDOs," Altemeyer explains how people with a high "Social Dominance Orientation"—that is, authoritarian leadership traits—complicate the picture:

Remember a few lines ago when I said high RWAs seemed to be the most prejudiced group ever found? Well, they lost the title when Felicia Pratto and Jim Sidanius began studying social dominators.

Elsewhere, in articles with titles such as "Why Do Religious Fundamentalists Tend to Be Prejudiced?" and "A Revised Religious Fundamentalism Scale: The Short and Sweet of It," Altemeyer uses a mixture of provocation, clarity, and humor to get his readers interested in sociological and psychological issues that are controversial, complex, and deeply serious.

In some science journals, and particularly in medical research, the colon may introduce a "type of study" subtitle that usefully supplements the main title:

- "Geriatric Care Management for Low-Income Seniors: A Randomised Controlled Trial" [Medicine]
- "Safety of the RTS,S/AS02D Candidate Malaria Vaccine in Infants Living in a Highly Endemic Area of Mozambique: A Double Blind Randomised Controlled Phase I/IIb Trial" [Medicine]

All too often, however, titular colons perform no obviously useful function aside from allowing an author, in effect, to cram two titles into one:

- "Integration of the Research Library Service into the Editorial Process: 'Embedding' the Librarian into the Media" [Computer Science]
- "Multistate Characters and Diet Shifts: Evolution of Erotylidae (Coleoptera)" [Evolutionary Biology]
- "Scaffolding through the Network: Analysing the Promotion of Improved Online Scaffolds among University Students" [Higher Education]

The advantage of these double-barreled "informative: informative" titles is that they pack a lot of content into a small space. A major disadvantage is that they often end up being twice as long-winded, jargon-laden, and abstract as a single-barreled title: that is, twice as "academic" rather than twice as inviting.

For academic authors who aspire to write engaging *and* informative titles, the colon is an undeniably useful device. A much trickier challenge is to combine—like Dawkins with his distracted bees—catchy and descriptive elements within a single, colon-free phrase. There are many ways to accomplish such a splicing. For example, the title might ask a question:

- "What Color Is the Sacred?" [Cultural Studies]
- "What Do Faculty and Students Really Think about E-books?" [Computer Science]

Or set a scene:

- "When Parents Want Children to Stay Home for College" [Higher Education]
- "The Riddle of Hiram Revels" [Law]

Or offer a challenging statement of fact or opinion:

- "Queen Promiscuity Lowers Disease within Honeybee Colonies" [Evolutionary Biology]
- "Why Killing Some People Is More Seriously Wrong than Killing Others" [Philosophy]

Or invoke a metaphor:

- "Rooting the Tree of Life Using Nonubiquitous Genes" [Evolutionary Biology]
- "The Specter of Hegel in Coleridge's *Biographia Literaria*" [History]

Or create an unexpected juxtaposition:

- "The Foreign Policy of the Calorie" [History]

Or make a claim so grand and compelling that we cannot help but want to read further:

- "Against Darwinism" [Philosophy]
- "Comprehending Envy" [Psychology]

In all of the above examples, the authors have found graceful and compact ways to frame their research subjects without resorting to a colon.

Some academics will argue, however, that the brevity and breeziness of such titles come at an unacceptable cost. How, they ask, will fellow researchers know what an article is *about* if its title lacks relevant subject keywords? This is where the paratext comes into play. An article cryptically titled "Hors d'oeuvre," for example, becomes considerably less opaque when we learn that it appeared in a journal called *Eighteenth-Century Studies* as part of a special issue on "Derrida and the Eighteenth Century"; pun-loving devotees of the French literary theorist Jacques Derrida will immediately deduce that the article offers an intellectual tasting platter (hors d'oeuvre = appetizer) to readers interested in noncanonical aspects of Derrida's writing (hors d'oeuvre = "outside the work"). Thanks to recent advances in electronic search technologies, titles no longer provide the only or even the principal means by which researchers in many disciplines locate relevant articles. Yet academics remain shackled to the notion that titles must always include major keywords. Roughly 80 percent of the articles in the journal *Social Networks,* for instance, contain the word "network" or "networking" in their titles.

Cultural theorist Marjorie Garber notes that "for a journalist to describe a scholarly book as 'academic' is to say that it is abstruse, dull, hard to read, and probably not worth the trouble of getting through"; conversely, for an academic to describe a scholarly book as "journalistic" is to say that it lacks "hard analysis, complexity, or deep thought."[8] The same tension applies, on a microcosmic scale, to scholarly titles. A "journalistic" title—one deliberately designed to attract the reader's attention, in the manner of a newspaper headline or magazine feature—operates for many academics as a marker of intellectual shallowness, whether or not the content of the work bears out that prejudice. Yet a worthy, pedestrian title offers no compensatory guarantee of research quality. Indeed, a formulaic title carries a potentially crippling subtext: "I am a formulaic thinker." And formulaic thinkers, by and large, are not the ones who set the world on fire with their research innovations.

PHILIP WADLER

Scientists often insist that serious science demands serious titles. Yet computer scientist Philip Wadler and his colleagues in the functional programming community (R. B. Findler, S. P. Jones, R. Lämmel, S. Lindley, S. Marlow, M. Odersky, E. Runne, and J. Yallop, among others) clearly believe otherwise. Their titles range from the humorous to the whimsical:

- "Well-Typed Programs Can't Be Blamed"
- "Making a Fast Curry: Push/Enter vs. Eval/Apply for Higher-Order Languages"
- "Scrap Your Boilerplate: A Practical Design Pattern for Generic Programming"
- "Et tu, XML? The Downfall of the Relational Empire"
- "Two Ways to Bake Your Pizza—Translating Parameterised Types into Java"
- "Idioms Are Oblivious, Arrows Are Meticulous, Monads Are Promiscuous"

These punning titles are not merely empty window dressing; rather, they reflect a deep-seated belief in the power of language to advance innovative thinking. Evocative title words such as *blame, deforestation,* and *pizza* are part of Wadler's everyday programming lexicon: the notion of *blame,* for example, allows programmers to show that "when more-typed and less-typed portions of a program interact . . . any type failures are due to the less-typed portion"; *deforestation* is "an algorithm that transforms programs to eliminate intermediate trees"; and *Pizza* is a functional language that incorporates Java (see http://homepages.inf.ed.ac.uk/wadler/).

Like Murray Gell-Mann, the Nobel Prize–winning physicist who coined the word "quark" based on a line from James Joyce's *Finnegans Wake,* Wadler and his colleagues are scientists with a sense of humor. Far from undercutting the seriousness of their research, their playful titles offer evidence of highly creative minds at work.

THINGS TO TRY

- What first impression do you want to make on your chosen audience? Remember, your title announces your intention to be serious, humorous, detailed, expansive, technical, or accessible—possibly several of those things at once. Double-check that your title matches your intention.

- Take a look at the publication list on your curriculum vitae. How many of your past titles contain colons? In each case, can you clearly articulate your reason for needing both a title and a subtitle?

- If you use colons frequently, try crafting a colon-free title. As an extra challenge, see if you can come up with a colon-free title that is both engaging and informative.

- If you seldom or never use colons, or if your titles are informative but not engaging, try out the "catchy: descriptive" trick. First, formulate a snappy but appropriate title (for example, "Snakes on a Plane") to go with your not-so-snappy descriptive subtitle ("Aggressive Serpentine Behavior in a Restrictive Aeronautical Environment"). Next, ask yourself whether your title would still make sense without the subtitle. In some situations—for instance, a disciplinary conference or a special issue of a journal, where the context may supply all the extra information that is needed—you might find you can get away with just "Snakes on a Plane" after all.

- Identify some typical titles in your discipline and analyze their grammatical structure: for example, "The Development of Efficacy in Teams: A Multilevel and Longitudinal Perspective" becomes *The Abstract Noun of Abstract Noun in Plural Collective Noun: An Adjective and Adjective Abstract Noun.* Now see if you can come up with a title that does *not* use those predictable structures.

- For inspiration, find an engaging title from a discipline other than your own and mimic its structure. No one in your discipline need ever know.

- A few more tricks for constructing an engaging (or at least better-than-boring) title:

  - Make sure your title contains no more than one or two abstract or collective nouns. (Many academic titles contain seven, eight, or more!) Abstract nouns *(analysis, structure, development, education)* and collective nouns *(students, teachers, patients, subjects)* have a generic, lulling quality, particularly when they occur in journals where the same noun is used frequently, as in a criminology journal where most of the titles contain the nouns *crime* and *criminology.*
  - Avoid predictable "academic verbs," especially in participle form: for example, *preparing, promoting, enforcing* (law); *engaging, applying, improving* (higher education); *rethinking, reopening, overcoming* (history); *predicting, relating, linking* (evolutionary biology).
  - Include one or two words that you would not expect to find in any other title in the same journal. Concrete nouns *(piano, guppy, path)* and vivid verbs *(ban, mutilate, gestate)* are particularly effective. Proper nouns (*Wagner, London, Phasianus colchicus*) can also help individualize your title and ground your research in a specific time and place.

CHAPTER 7

HOOKS AND SINKERS

We were somewhere around Barstow on the edge of the desert when the drugs began to take hold. I remember saying something like "I feel a bit lightheaded; maybe you should drive . . ." And suddenly there was a terrible roar all around us and the sky was full of what looked like huge bats, all swooping and screeching and diving around the car, which was going about a hundred miles an hour with the top down to Las Vegas. And a voice was screaming: "Holy Jesus! What are these goddamn animals?"[1]

If the drug trip described in the opening lines of *Fear and Loathing in Las Vegas* had transported Hunter S. Thompson beyond the California desert to the even more bizarre and alien landscape of academe, his account might instead be titled *Hallucinogen-Induced Anxiety Disorders and Revulsion Responses in a Southwestern Gambling-Oriented Locality: A Qualitative Study,* and the first few sentences would read something like this:

It has been suggested that frontal brain asymmetry (FBA) is associated with differences in fundamental dimensions of emotion (Davidson, 2002). According to the directional model of negative affect, the left prefrontal cortex is associated with the approach-related emotion, anger, whereas the right prefrontal area is associated with the withdrawal-related emotion, anxiety.

Of course, we all know that scientific researchers are supposed to be concerned with serious, sober matters such as frontal brain asymmetry, not with drug-fueled road trips and hallucinated bats. (The actual title of the article quoted above, by the way, is "Anticipatory Anxiety-Induced Changes in Human Lateral Prefrontal Cortex Activity.") All the same, academics who care about good writing could do worse than to study the opening moves of novelists and journalists, who generally know a thing or two about how to capture an audience's attention.

Not every engaging academic book, article, or chapter begins with an opening hook, but a striking number of them do. Stylish writers understand that if you are still reading three pages later, they have probably got you for the long haul. By contrast, nothing sinks a piece of prose more efficiently than a leaden first paragraph. In the sciences and social sciences, researchers frequently follow a four-step rhetorical sequence identified by John Swales as "Creating a Research Space," or CARS:

- Move 1: Establish that your particular area of research has some significance.
- Move 2: Selectively summarize the relevant previous research.
- Move 3: Show that the reported research is not complete.
- Move 4: Turn the gap into the research space for the present article.[2]

Promoted by Swales as a more subtle alternative to the conventional "problem-solution" model, this approach can help authors marshal a clear and compelling argument. However, the CARS model also has a lot to answer for. Move 1 encourages authors to begin with a sweeping statement of the obvious:

Ecologists and anthropologists, among others, recognize that humans have significantly affected the biophysical environment. [Anthropology]

SHANTHI AMERATUNGA

In 2002, an estimated 1–2 million people were killed and 50 million injured in road-traffic crashes worldwide, costing the global community about US$518 billion. The International Federation of Red Cross and Red Crescent Societies has described the situation as "a worsening global disaster destroying lives and livelihoods, hampering development and leaving millions in greater vulnerability." Without appropriate action, road-traffic injuries are predicted to escalate from the ninth leading contributor to the global burden of disease in 1990 to the third by 2020. . . . In this Review, we aim to summarise the characteristics of the rise in road-traffic injuries and present an evidence based approach to prevent road-traffic crashes. Our Review uses the substantial work undertaken by international experts contributing to the 2004 world report and data published since that time.

In the opening lines of this review article from *The Lancet*, population health researcher Shanthi Ameratunga and her colleagues Martha Hijar and Robyn Norton demonstrate that the CARS (Creating a Research Space) model can work well when employed gracefully, generously, and without exaggeration. Rather than baldly asserting the importance of the topic, they offer hard evidence about global death rates, injury numbers, and monetary costs. And rather than claiming to overturn or better the research of distinguished colleagues, the authors acknowledge and build on "the substantial work undertaken by international experts." Note also their use of active, concrete verbs *(kill, injure, cost, predict, escalate, prevent, highlight)* and their canny choice of a supporting quotation from Red Cross/Red Crescent that contains language as vivid and precise as their own *(worsening, disaster, destroying, hampering, vulnerability)*.

There is, to be sure, still plenty of scope here for the authors to tighten up their prose. In their penultimate sentence, for example, "an evidence based approach to prevent road-traffic crashes" could be more elegantly rephrased as "an evidence-based approach to preventing road-traffic crashes," and the words "aim to" could be deleted altogether. For stylish academic writers, the work of editing and polishing is never done.

Move 2 often leads to egregious name-dropping rather than
meaningful engagement with colleagues' ideas and arguments:

> Identity is central to any sociocultural account of learning. As far as
> mathematics is concerned, it is essential to students' beliefs about
> themselves as learners and as potential mathematicians (Klooster-
> man & Coughan, 1994; Carlson, 1999; Martino & Maher, 1999;
> Boaler & Greeno, 2000; De Corte et al., 2002; Maher, 2005), and it
> has vital gender, race and class components (see Becker, 1995; Bur-
> ton, 1995; Bartholomew, 1999; Cooper, 2001; Dowling, 2001; Kas-
> sem, 2001; Boaler, 2002; Cobb & Hodge, 2002; Gilborn & Mirza,
> 2002; Nasir, 2002; De Abreu & Cline, 2003; Black, 2004). [Higher
> Education]

Move 3 invites authors to take a crowbar to the existing literature, jimmying open alleged research gaps whether or not they
actually exist:

> Although scholars have demonstrated the link between collective ef-
> ficacy and team performance (Gully, Incalcaterra, Joshi & Beaubien,
> 2002), little is yet known about the factors responsible for the devel-
> opment of collective efficacy. [Psychology]

Finally, with Move 4, the author steps boldly into the breach,
making claims, frequently inflated, for the novelty and importance of his or her own research:

> This study expands the existing models for estimating the effect of
> community college attendance on baccalaureate attainment by map-
> ping out the points of divergence in the educational trajectory
> of 2-year and 4-year students. [Higher Education]

Developed to encourage rhetorical precision, the CARS method
frequently steers authors into rhetorical predictability instead.

In some academic contexts, formulaic openings are required;
in most, however, they are merely conventional. Philosopher
Jonathan Wolff notes that students in his discipline are trained
"to give the game away right from the start. A detective novel
written by a good philosophy student would begin: 'In this novel

I shall show that the butler did it.' "[3] A quick trawl through several top philosophy journals confirms that up-front openings are indeed a disciplinary norm:

> In this essay I argue that citizens of a liberal-democratic state, one that I argue has a morally justified claim to political authority, enjoy a moral right to engage in acts of suitably constrained civil disobedience, or what I will call a moral right to public disobedience.

Yet these same journals also reveal that many other options are available to philosophers who resist the "butler did it" trend. An article on the mind-body problem, for example, opens with a carefully chosen literary quotation:

> "Merely—you are my own nose."
> The Nose regarded the major and contracted its brows a little.
> "My dear sir, you speak in error" was its reply. "I am just myself—myself separately." Gogol (1835)

An essay on feminism and pornography begins with a question drawn from a newspaper story:

> A recent article in *The Boston Globe* asks, "What happened to the anti-porn feminists?"

A study of corporate responsibility catches our attention with a historical anecdote:

> The Herald of Free Enterprise, a ferry operating in the English Channel, sank on March 6, 1987, drowning nearly two hundred people. The official inquiry found that the company running the ferry was extremely sloppy, with poor routines of checking and management.

And a paper about the problem of mental causation starts by painting a vividly personalized picture of physical pain:

> Quincy strikes his thumb with a hammer, feels pain, and dances in circles. Quincy's pain, we think, causes his dancing, but can it? Quincy's pain depends on some activity in his brain—say, his C-fibers firing—

RICHARD DAWKINS

I have just listened to a lecture in which the topic for discussion was the fig. Not a botanical lecture, a literary one. We got the fig in literature, the fig as metaphor, changing perceptions of the fig, the fig as emblem of pudenda and the fig leaf as modest concealer of them, "fig" as an insult, the social construction of the fig, D. H. Lawrence on how to eat a fig in society, "reading fig" and, I rather think, "the fig as text." The speaker's final pensée was the following. He recalled to us the Genesis story of Eve tempting Adam to eat of the fruit of the tree of knowledge. Genesis doesn't specify, he reminded us, which fruit it was. Traditionally, people take it to be an apple. The lecturer suspected that actually it was a fig, and with this piquant little shaft he ended his talk. . . . But our elegant lecturer was missing so much. There is a genuine paradox and real poetry lurking in the fig, with subtleties to exercise an inquiring mind and wonders to uplift an aesthetic one. In this book I want to move to a position where I can tell the true story of the fig.

With these opening lines from *Climbing Mount Improbable*, evolutionary biologist Richard Dawkins uses just about every rhetorical trick in the book to hook and hold our attention: humor, metaphor, concrete nouns, active verbs, varied sentence length, literary references, and more. He begins by placing us directly in the moment: "I have just listened to a lecture." With a few well-chosen words, he constructs a breezy précis of what he has just heard: "We got the fig in literature, the fig as metaphor." Dawkins's lightly sarcastic tone—"I rather think," "the speaker's final pensée," "this piquant little shaft"—risks turning some readers off. But his offer to tell us the *true* story of the fig, an emblem of evolutionary improbability at its most intriguing and bizarre, will keep most of us turning the pages.

and those firings cause the muscles in his legs to move. If his neurons cause his legs to move, what more is there for his pain to do?

The authors of all four articles subsequently go on to state a thesis ("here's my main argument") and carve out a research space ("here's how my work contributes to the existing literature")—but only after having secured their readers' attention with a relevant quotation, question, story, or illustration.

Every discipline has its own typical opening moves, which can provide a rich store of ideas and inspiration to academics in other fields. Historians often begin their articles by recounting a specific event that is exemplary of the period or problem they wish to explore:

> In 1924, a farmer named Kwadjo Agbanyamane and his mother borrowed £20 from a neighbor to buy some land near Peki, in the Gold Coast region of what is now Ghana. In return, Kwadjo "gave" the neighbor his six-year-old brother Kwamin, "to serve for the debt until" he could pay for the land.

Literary scholars like to spin webs of signification from a single starting quotation or anecdote:

> *Since our concern was speech, and speech impelled us*
> *To purify the dialect of the tribe*
> *And urge the mind to aftersight and foresight.* (T. S. Eliot)

> The concern of this article is language, and specifically the various projects of linguistic "purification" that were part of literary modernism in Britain.

Popular science writers may home in on a fascinating fact: a creature, object, or phenomenon that captures our imagination but then leads the author into a discussion of wider issues.

Any opening gambit can, of course, become stale and predictable if used repetitively or unimaginatively. However, alert stylists will find ways to keep their openings fresh. Literary historian Stephen Greenblatt recommends that writers "plunge the reader into a story that has already begun" and create "the desire to know

STEPHEN GREENBLATT

Several years ago at Harvard, a friend invited me to dinner and asked if I would pick up two of his other guests, Nadine Gordimer and Carlos Fuentes. Thrilled, I readily agreed to do so. On the appointed evening, all dressed up and tingling with pleasant anticipation, I went first to get Nadine Gordimer, who immediately deflated me somewhat by getting into the backseat of my car. My feeble attempts at small talk went nowhere. When I picked up Carlos Fuentes a few minutes later, he turned out to know Gordimer—there was a flurry of kissing on both cheeks—and so naturally he too got into the backseat. As I headed off toward Newton, half amused and half annoyed, the conversation between my two distinguished passengers encapsulated the globalization of literature.

Literary historian Stephen Greenblatt opens this article on racial memory and literary history with a self-deprecating personal anecdote. Deftly recounting his own amusement and discomfort at being reduced to the role of chauffeur for Gordimer and Fuentes, he pulls his readers right into the car with him as he eavesdrops on two of the most eminent authors in the Western world. Greenblatt's slightly over-the-top vocabulary—*thrilled, all dressed up, tingling, flurry*—cues us to the multiple layers of irony in his narrative. Later in the same paragraph, the self-confessed "feeble" conversationalist gets the last laugh by turning his sharp critical lens on his two passengers.

Greenblatt himself is the first to acknowledge that stylishness can shade into solipsism if writers focus only on themselves. Far from advocating scholarly navel-gazing, he urges academic writers to carry their "passionate energies into an alien world":

I am suggesting only that you should try to write well—and that means bringing to the table all of your alertness, your fears, and your desires. And every once in a while—say, every third paper—tell yourself that you will take a risk.

more." Himself a master of the technique, Greenblatt notes that he used to open all his academic essays with a historical anecdote attached to a date, for example: "In September 1580, as he passed through a small French town on his way to Switzerland and Italy, Montaigne was told an unusual story that he duly recorded in his travel journal." Eventually, however, the formula became "a bit too familiar in my writing, so I decided to stop."[4] Now Greenblatt favors personal anecdotes instead.

An effective first paragraph need not be flashy, gimmicky, or even provocative. It must, however, make the reader want to keep reading. Compare the following openings, both from articles published in the same biology journal. The first begins with an attention-getting question and then segues to a specific case study framed in clear, concrete language. The second, by contrast, freights a potentially intriguing topic with ponderous abstractions:

> Many ecological studies are inspired by Hutchinson's simple question, "Why are there so many kinds of animals?" . . . Communities of ants, well known for being structured by competition, provide an excellent testing ground for the mechanisms that can promote coexistence.
>
> The conspicuous interspecific variability of the mammalian penis has long been of value as a taxonomic tool (e.g., Hooper and Musser 1964a, 1964b), though as in other animal groups the selective pressures underlying such genitalic diversity have not been well understood.

Amazingly, the authors of the first article make the study of ant communities sound fascinating, while the author of the second succeeds in rendering penis size one of the most boring topics on earth.

In my data sample of academic articles from across the disciplines, I found that roughly 25 percent of the articles open in a deliberately engaging way, offering stories, anecdotes, scene-setting descriptions of historical events or artistic representations, literary or historical quotations, or provocative questions aimed directly at the reader (see Figure 2.1 in Chapter 2). The other 75 percent begin with an informational statement of some kind; that is, a sentence that announces the topic of the article, presents relevant background information, summarizes previous research, posits a fact, makes a claim for the importance of the topic, or sets up the author's main thesis, either by identifying a gap in existing knowledge or by presenting the opening moves of a "straw man" argument ("Most people think that. . . . but this paper will show otherwise"). As one might expect, humanities scholars proved far more likely than scientists or social scientists to start with a deliberately engaging opening. Notably, however, with the exception of medicine, every single discipline in my data sample includes at least one or two articles that begin with an opening hook—an indication that, in most academic journals, attention-grabbing openings are not illegal, merely uncommon. Social scientists, in particular, can draw courage from this statistic, which confirms that CARS in the first paragraph is not their only option. Like a catchy title, an opening hook communicates a powerful subtext: "I care about my readers, and I am willing to work hard to catch and hold their attention."

THINGS TO TRY

- Ask yourself the same questions that you asked when considering your title: What kind of first impression do you want to make on your audience? Does your opening move match your intention?
- Find an article or book chapter that particularly engages you and analyze its opening structure. What *specific* opening strategies does the author use? Can you adapt those strategies for your own work?
- Experiment with one or more of the following opening ploys:
  - a literary quotation
  - a scholarly or historical quotation

- a personal anecdote
- a historical anecdote
- an anecdote drawn from your research
- a description of a scene or artwork
- a dialog or conversation
- a surprising fact
- a direct admonition to the audience ("Consider this"; "Imagine that")
- a challenging question

  If you do decide to start with an attention-grabbing hook, however, make sure it speaks to the content and purpose of your article or chapter.
- Instead of a hook, construct a funnel: an opening paragraph that draws in your reader with a compelling statement of the topic's importance and then narrows down to your main argument. Better yet, start with a hook that pulls your reader into the mouth of the funnel.

CHAPTER 8

THE STORY NET

A carefully woven opening paragraph will catch no readers if, on the very next page, you slacken the net and let all the fish go. Stylish writers know the importance of sustaining a compelling *story* rather than merely sprinkling isolated anecdotes throughout an otherwise sagging narrative. A book or article that supplies no suspense, no narrative arc, and no sense of moving from A to B will not hold the reader's attention nearly as effectively as an article plotted, even at the most subtle level, like a good thriller ("What will happen next?") or a mystery novel ("What clues will the intrepid researcher/detective unearth?") or a bildungsroman ("What lessons will the protagonist learn along the way, and from whom?").

Literary scholar Brian Boyd has argued that all artistic activity, including our love of storytelling, can be traced to deep-seated evolutionary impulses: since long before the dawn of literacy, human beings have used stories to attract attention, convey information, persuade doubters, solve problems, build communities, and make sense of the world.[1] Researchers vying for prestigious grants are often acutely aware that their success depends on their ability to tell a good story, and scholars in disciplines as diverse as anthropology, sociology, education, law, management, and medicine have advocated and theorized storytelling both as research methodology and professional practice.[2]

Yet relatively few scientists and social scientists have been trained in the art of crafting a compelling narrative, while humanities scholars who work in textually rich fields such as literature, history, or law often bury their own best stories under layers of abstraction and critical theory.

Every research project is made up of stories—the researcher's story, the research story, the stories of individual subjects and participants, the backstory—each of which contains various plot twists of its own. For stylish academic writers, then, the fundamental question to ask is not "Do I have a story to tell?" but "*Which* story or stories do I want to tell, and how can I tell them most effectively?" In fiction and drama, a story typically revolves around a protagonist who faces a problem or obstacle of some kind: a lost father, an indifferent beloved, an unsolved mystery, a ring that will cause unspeakable evil unless it is thrown into the heart of a fiery mountain. The researcher's story, likewise, always involves a character with a problem: that is, a scholar who poses a research question, collects evidence, forms a theory, and sets out to persuade the reader that this theory is correct. In the following examples, randomly selected from my data sample, the research question frames the researcher's (or researchers') story:

- Law/Criminology

  - *Research Question:* How does procedural justice influence public perceptions of the police in Australia?
  - *Researchers' Story:* The researchers analyze data from a large public survey in Australia, compare the results to similar data from the United States, and conclude that "people who believe police use procedural justice when they exercise their authority are more likely to view police as legitimate, and in turn are more satisfied with police services."

- Evolutionary Biology

  - *Research Question:* Why do birds migrate?
  - *Researchers' Story:* The research team reviews previous studies of bird migration, discusses their shortcomings, and

LORD ALFRED DENNING

It happened on 19th April 1964. It was bluebell time in Kent.

With these evocative words, British justice Lord Alfred Denning opened his famous legal judgment *Hinz v. Berry*, which upheld the award of substantial legal damages to a mother of nine whose husband had been killed during a family picnic by the driver of an out-of-control Jaguar. Lord Denning was a master storyteller who understood the importance of plot, character, and setting. Sometimes he focused on a protagonist's defining characteristics:

Old Peter Beswick was a coal merchant in Eccles, Lancashire. He had no business premises. All he had was a lorry, scales, and weights.

Sometimes he used literary devices such as assonance and alliteration to color his descriptions:

This is a case of a barmaid who was badly bitten by a big dog.

Sometimes he appealed, directly and shamelessly, to the audience's emotions:

In summertime village cricket is the delight of everyone. Nearly every village has its own cricket field where the young men play and the old men watch. In the village of Lintz in County Durham they have their own ground, where they have played these last 70 years. They tend it well. . . . Yet now after these 70 years a judge of the High Court has ordered that they must not play there any more. He has issued an injunction to stop them. He has done it at the instance of a newcomer who is no lover of cricket.

To critics who object to such blatant emotional manipulation, Denning would no doubt have replied that the law exists to regulate human behavior and that all human behavior involves emotion. To deny the power of story is to suppress our own humanity.

uses a new approach to test and refine "the evolutionary precursor hypothesis" developed by earlier researchers.

- Literary Studies
  - *Research Question:* How did the popularity of recorded sound devices such as the pianola and gramophone shape early twentieth-century poetry and poetics?
  - *Researcher's Story:* The researcher reads about the history of the pianola, trawls the literature of the period for references to recorded music, and constructs a series of persuasive close readings mediated by Schopenhauer's and Helmholtz's writings on the relationship between music and memory.

Some scholars turn the researcher's story into a central feature of their work, as when cultural historian Judith Pascoe structures an entire book around her quest for a single unrecoverable piece of knowledge: what did the famous eighteenth-century actress Sarah Siddons really sound like?[3] But even when the researcher's story does not feature directly in a scholarly book or article, there are many other academic venues where it may be told to good effect: for example, in a public lecture, a student seminar, a grant application, a book preface, or the opening chapter of a PhD thesis. Whether as a framing device or as a tale in its own right, the researcher's story can create a sympathetic bond between the author and the audience by showing the human side of academic endeavor.

The research story, on the other hand, is the story that the researcher uncovers, analyzes, or otherwise recounts but does not participate in directly. Embedded within both the researcher's story and the research story are the individual stories of research subjects and the backstory of the research. Academics can add drama and interest to the research story by panning to other stories from time to time. For instance, the criminologists could open their article with an anecdote about an innocent citizen unexpectedly caught up in a police search (an individual story that illustrates the relevance and immediacy of their research); the biologists could give a brief account of previous scholarly debates about bird migration (the backstory of the research); and the literary scholar could single out a particular historical event, such as the late nineteenth-century craze for public piano bashing, and analyze its significance within the larger story of modernist cultural production (an individual story that also helps fill in the backstory).

Novelist E. M. Forster famously described a *story* as "a narrative of events arranged in their time sequence," whereas a *plot* "is also a narrative of events, the emphasis falling on causality"; thus, according to Forster, "The king died and then the queen died" is a story, whereas "The king died, and then the queen died *of grief*" is a plot. A story tells you what happened; a plot tells you why.[4] Like novelists, stylish academic writers transform stories into plots through careful attention to elements such as character, setting, point of view, and narrative sequence. In the researcher's story, the potential human characters include the researcher and all the other people he or she encounters along the way: research team members, skeptical colleagues, and previous researchers in the field whose theories are being built upon or overturned. In the research story, the main characters might be humans (for example, police), animals (for example, migratory birds), or even ideas (for example, modernist conceptions of memory). Historian of science Robert Root-Bernstein records numerous examples of famous scientists who have imagined themselves as animals, atoms, or other natural phenomena:

With each animal I studied I *became* that animal. [Desmond Morris, ethology]

What did the carbon atom *want* to do? [Peter Debye, chemistry]

[I gained] a feeling of how I would behave if I were a certain alloy. [Cyril Stanley Smith, metallurgy]

Instead of treating hydromagnetic equations I prefer to sit and ride on each electron and ion and try to imagine what the world is like from its point of view. [Hans Alfvin, physics]

SALLY BANES

When I lived in the SoHo area of New York City, working as a dance and performance art critic in the late 1970s and early 1980s, I was a frequent visitor to the Kitchen Center for Music, Video, and Dance. Recently, while in New York to dig through the Kitchen's archives in preparation for this article, I saw their production of Ann Carlson's *Night Light*. This site-specific performance was a social archaeology of a neighborhood in the form of an artful walking tour through the streets of the Chelsea area, between Greenwich Village and midtown, where the Kitchen has been located since 1985, punctuated by a series of frozen tableaux recreating historic photographs of Chelsea incidents. Afterwards, we all reconvened at the Kitchen to drink beer and chat with the tour guides and performers in the downstairs performance space.

Performance scholar Sally Banes imbues her academic writing with a dancer's physicality and a storyteller's sense of place. The evocative title of this article, "Choreographing Community: Dancing in the Kitchen," prepares us for its highly concrete opening paragraph, in which Banes manages to introduce the Kitchen Center in SoHo, describe her own project of "digging through" its archives, take us on a walking tour of the neighborhood, and finally bring us back to the Kitchen for a beer. By the time she moves on to abstract concepts such as the center's gradual transition from "a constituency of artists to a constituency of audiences," Banes has made us eager to hear the full story.

Elsewhere, in an article titled "Olfactory Performances," Banes involves our senses in a very different way, describing recent theatrical productions that incorporate the smell of cooking food:

bread, toast, bacon and eggs, hamburgers, soup, spaghetti sauce, omelettes, popcorn, onions, garlic, artichokes, mushrooms, panela (caramelized cane sugar), hazelnut cookies, risotto, jasmine-scented rice, fish and chips, curry, sausages, sauerkraut and kielbasa, kidneys, boiled beef, Cajun shrimp, and Australian barbequed meats of all kinds.

Hungry yet?

I actually felt as if I were right down there and these [chromosomes] were my friends. [Barbara McClintock, cytogenetics][5]

Abstract concepts, likewise, can be conceptualized as characters in a drama, complete with romantic attractions and fatal flaws. What obstacles do they overcome? What transformations do they undergo?

Physical settings seldom figure explicitly in academic writing, especially in disciplines where researchers have been trained to regard their work as the revelation of timeless truths. Yet the stories we remember best are often set in distinctive physical landscapes, whether real or imagined: the fairy-tale castle, the woodcutter's cottage, the steep road through the mountain pass. The researcher's story and the research story offer many potential settings, from the laboratory where an important scientific experiment took place to the small island where a rare species of flightless bird evolved. Sometimes a few lines are all it takes to sketch a scene that will linger in the reader's mind:

1987. New Zealand. A warm, stuffy room in an old school building. A group of mathematics teachers have been working for a week discussing mathematics education for the indigenous Maori people. . . . They are trying to explain the difference between continuous and discrete data to a Maori elder. Examples are given: heights and shoe sizes; temperatures and football scores; time and money.[6]

The day of dedication, 11 November 1934, was overcast. . . . The clouds parted as the wreath was laid. . . . This eerie and sudden appearance of a sunbeam exactly faithful to a time and place distilled the essence of centuries of inspired viewing within the cathedral observatories.[7]

This trouble started when I began searching in earnest for a methodological framework that encouraged me to write richly of my experience. . . . I found autoethnography late one evening in the quiet of the university library.[8]

Each of these descriptions—by mathematics educator Bill Barton, historian John Heilbron, and academic developer Tai Peseta, respectively—includes evocative concrete details: the stuffy room, the sunbeam piercing the clouds, the quiet library where the researcher experiences an intellectual epiphany.

For writers of fiction, point of view is another essential consideration: through whose eyes do we watch the story unfold? A novel or short story might have a naïve first-person narrator whose innocence shapes our perceptions (as in Mark Twain's *Huckleberry Finn*); an omniscient, gently ironic narrator who sees into all the characters' minds (as in Charles Dickens's *Oliver Twist*); a narrator who tells us he is sane, but whose actions reveal him to be otherwise (as in Edgar Allan Poe's *The Telltale Heart*); a series of narrators who present radically different viewpoints (as in William Faulkner's *The Sound and the Fury*); or even an unreliable narrator who earns the reader's trust but turns out to be withholding crucial information (as in Agatha Christie's *The Murder of Roger Ackroyd*).[9] Academic writers often strive to convey a completely neutral perspective; as merchants of truth rather than fiction, we see it as our job to inform our readers, not to play with their expectations or their minds. Yet that neutrality, when examined closely, turns out to be something of a myth. All academics are partisans, after all, arguing for the validity of our theories, the accuracy of our data, and the strategic importance of our own narrow neck of the research woods. The question "Whose point of view am I *really* representing here?" can help us keep our biases in check. Other, related questions—"Whose point of view do I *want* to represent?" "What other points of view am I suppressing or neglecting?"—remind us that our own research stories will be enriched rather than weakened by the inclusion of dissenting voices.

Narrative structure, a consideration that operates within and around other structural elements such as chapters and sections, refers to the order in which a story gets told. In Forster's example

PETER CLOUGH

My problem with Molly is not that he lacks words, but rather that they can spill out of him with a wild, fairground pulse: they are sparklers, he waves them splashing around him. And my other problem with Molly's words is that many of them are not very nice; they are squibs that make you jump out of the way. For the moment I think that they are my only problems.

With "Molly," the story of a delinquent child and the teacher who tries in vain to save him, educator Peter Clough offers an emotionally wrenching case study that helps its readers understand how easily the product of a dysfunctional family can slip through the cracks of the British school system. The catch—one that will give many researchers pause—is that Molly is not a real boy. Both he and the narrator are composite fictional characters created by Clough to communicate the "deeper truths" of professional and personal experience. To "tell the truth as one sees it," Clough believes, sometimes "data may have to be manipulated to serve that larger purpose."

For some academics, Clough's defense of data manipulation is indefensible. His whole scholarly project, however, is "to rattle the bars which I see *any* given social science methods as throwing up around attempts to characterise experience." Clough's argument is twofold. First, he encourages researchers to tell stories that hold our attention, help us make sense of the world, and validate the "vitally constitutive role of language" in constructing knowledge. Second, he questions the supremacy of social science methodologies that suppress personal engagement: "Despite the sterility of the instruments, we never come innocent to a research task." Through the power of fiction, Clough explores "the ethnographer's dilemma—the conscious theft of glimpses of people's lives in the interests of research."

of a plot—"The king died, and then the queen died of grief"—the storyteller could start with the death of the king and move forward from there, or roll back the clock and begin with the backstory of the king and queen's early courtship, or open the story with the death of the queen and then unspool the narrative through flashbacks that eventually return us to the present moment. Likewise, in an academic article, we could begin with the research question (the researcher's story) or with a brief historical account of previous research (the backstory) or with an example of how this research has changed lives (an individual story within the larger research story). The trick is to decide which part of the story you want to toss your readers into first, and then guide them forward from there.

The art of academic storytelling is a complex business, yet it depends on a very simple principle: a good story makes people want to keep reading to find out what happens next. A skillful academic writer can construct a compelling narrative whose main "character" is an institution (How did the University of X respond to the government's new funding regime?), a methodology (Why are scattergrams more effective than bar graphs in conveying information about cosmic rays?), or a technique (What happens to the quality of undergraduate student essays in a class where peer assessment is introduced as a marking strategy?). However, such narratives become even more powerful and persuasive when they include individual stories about, for example, the *employees* at the University of X, the *researchers* who employ the methodology, or the *students* who wrote the essays. And let's not forget the readers' stories: the various interests, experiences, and biases that our audience brings to the party.

THINGS TO TRY

- Make a list of all the potential *characters* in your research story, including nonhuman characters such as theories and ideas. For each character, jot down:

- a physical description (in the case of an intangible concept, try imagining how you would represent it as a cartoon character);
- a personality profile (strengths, flaws, motivations);
- an obstacle faced by the character;
- a transformation that the character will undergo.

- Briefly describe the various *settings* in which your research story takes place, and experiment with ways of invoking those physical details in your writing. For example, you could:

  - include an evocative place name in your title;
  - use your opening paragraph to set a scene;
  - provide a description of the setting in an illustrative anecdote or case study.

- Play around with *point of view*. What would your research story sound like if it were told by one of your research subjects, or by a rival researcher who disagrees with your theoretical framework, or by a nonhuman character in your story, such as a molecule, a migrating bird, or a theoretical framework? Can you incorporate some or all of these perspectives into your writing?

- Draw a map or blueprint of your *narrative structure*, and then see if you can come up with at least three alternative ways to tell your story: for example, by starting at the end rather than the beginning, by presenting a series of different points of view, or by withholding crucial details until the final section.

- Just for fun, choose a favorite book or movie, distill its plot into a single sentence, and imagine what would happen if you plotted your research story along the same lines, for example:

  - A murder mystery: The researcher/detective searches for clues, follows a few red herrings, and eventually

applies his or her superior deductive powers to solve the
mystery.

- *Hansel and Gretel:* The researcher's bold new theories get
  trapped in the cottage of an evil witch (a rival academic?)
  who wants to destroy them. However, they stage a crafty
  escape and emerge from the woods stronger and wiser than
  before.
- *Pride and Prejudice:* Two seemingly incompatible theoretical concepts are brought into a single conceptual space,
  where they dance, flirt, and argue passionately before
  eventually marrying and living happily ever after.
- *Rocky:* Against all odds, a scrappy, unproven methodology
  dukes it out against more-muscular opponents and eventually prevails, thanks to the unerring devotion of the faithful
  researcher.

Use insights gleaned from this exercise to breathe life into
your own research story.

CHAPTER 9

SHOW AND TELL

"Show, don't tell" is the mantra of the novelist, dramatist, and poet. Creative writers learn to convey key emotional information by means of physical details: the storyteller invokes primal terror by spinning a tale about a child alone in a dark forest; the poet represents the whole history of human grief with "an empty doorway and a maple leaf."[1] "Show *and* tell," in contrast, is the mantra of the stylish academic writer, who illuminates abstract ideas by grounding theory in practice and by anchoring abstract concepts in the real world.

As a starting point, nearly all stylish academic writers ply their readers with well-chosen *examples*, *examples*, and more *examples*. For example, philosophers Glyn Humphreys and Jane Riddoch open a highly technical article on action and perception by posing a provocative opening question immediately followed by an illustrative case in point:

> What is an object? . . . Consider watching someone walk behind a set of railings, a circumstance in which all the parts of their body are not visible at a given time. The lay answer, that the object is the person behind the railing, fails to account for how we see the fragmented parts of the person as a single "thing." How does our visual system construct the whole object, when the sensory evidence for the object is fragmentary?[2]

Without the image of a person walking behind a railing firmly planted in our minds, the authors' subsequent discussion of "bottom-up grouping," "familiarity-based grouping," and other key principles of Gestalt psychology would be considerably harder to follow, and their central argument—that our perception of discrete objects "depends on the actions we are programming and on the presence of action relations between stimuli"—would be much more difficult to grasp.

Anecdotes are examples drawn from real life, as when psycholinguist Steven Pinker illustrates the ideological power of grammar with two historical vignettes:

> In *1984* George Orwell has the state banning irregular verbs as a sign of its determination to crush the human spirit; in 1989 the writer of a personal ad in the *New York Review of Books* asked, "Are you an irregular verb?" as a sign of her determination to exalt it.[3]

An anecdote is, in essence, a miniature story, sometimes sketched in a sentence or two, sometimes spun out over several paragraphs. Not only do anecdotes effectively illustrate abstract concepts, they also satisfy our natural desire for narratives that feature human beings rather than merely ideas. A carefully placed anecdote can revive a reader's flagging attention and even inject some welcome humor into an otherwise sober academic discussion.

Case studies, likewise, draw us into stories about real people; they show and tell how theoretical concepts get played out in the world at large. In professionally oriented disciplines such as business, medicine, and education, entire academic journals—the *Journal of Business Case Studies,* the *Journal of Medical Case Reports,* the *Journal of Education Case Studies*—are devoted to the practice and discussion of case-based research methodologies. Academics in other, more theoretically oriented disciplines use case studies in less-rigorous but equally fruitful ways, anchoring and exemplifying larger arguments through attention to real-life situations. Philosopher and feminist geographer Gillian Rose uses home-based interviews with fourteen middle-class English

MICHAEL CORBALLIS

A few years ago I visited a publishing house in England and was greeted at the door by the manager, whose first words were: "We have a bit of a crisis. Ribena is trickling down the chandelier." I had never heard this sentence before but knew at once what it meant, and was soon able to confirm that it was true. For those who don't know, ribena is a red fruit drink that some people inflict on their children, and my first sinister thought was that the substance dripping from the chandelier was blood. It turned out that the room above was a crèche [day care], and one of the children had evidently decided that it would be more fun to pour her drink onto the floor than into her mouth.

In his book *From Hand to Mouth: The Origins of Language,* psycholinguist Michael Corballis offers this perfectly pitched anecdote—apt, unusual, humorous, and concrete—to illustrate "that language is not just a matter of learning associations between words":

I had never in my life encountered the words ribena and chandelier in the same sentence, or even in the remotest association with each other, yet I was immediately able to understand a sentence linking them.

Weaving "a story about the evolution of language from threads drawn from a broad range of disciplines," Corballis deploys a wide range of stylish techniques. He opens every chapter with a relevant example, illustration, or question. He chooses his words with care: "I am beguiled by the frivolous thought that we are descended, not from apes, but from birds." Even his chapter titles are eye-catching, memorable, and concrete: "Why Are We Lopsided?"; "Three Hands Better than Two?"

mothers to explore the role of family photographs in defining domestic space; Pacific studies scholars David Gegeo and Karen Ann Watson-Gegeo examine a specific rural development project in the Solomon Islands to reveal "how modernization, globalization, and older Anglo-European notions of community development continue to fail rural development in the Solomons"; organizational management experts Jeffrey Pfeffer and Tanya Menon analyze the disproportionately high "knowledge valuation" assigned to external business consultants by tracing the consultancy experiences of two different companies.[4] Through detailed analysis of specific situations, these authors make large, transferable claims about cultural identity formation, postcolonial rural development, and organizational knowledge, respectively.

A *scenario* functions very much like a case study, except that it depicts a fictional situation rather than a real one. Sometimes scenarios skate along the edge of satire, as when, in an article titled "Embodiment, Academics, and the Audit Culture," sports scientist Andrew Sparkes tells the funny but not so funny story of a "mythical (perhaps?) academic at an imaginary (perhaps?) university in England that is permeated by an audit culture." In the article's introduction, Sparkes explains that he based the "embodied struggles" of his tortured professor on "informal interviews with academics at various universities in England and selected personal experiences."[5] More realistic scenarios might explore the possible outcomes of an expected or likely sequence of events, such as global warming or nuclear war. (In some disciplines, such as climatology, *scenario* is in fact a technical term for computer-generated "what if" models.) The most effective scenarios, by and large, function much in the same way as anecdotes, examples, and case studies: they make abstract ideas concrete and imaginable. However, a scenario can invite ridicule if it proves too unlikely or outlandish, as when philosophers concerned with the ethics of abortion write about "hypothetical women impregnated by flying insects and the like," or when a theoretical physicist opens a report on how to increase a farmer's

BRIAN BOYD

In a game that asked us to associate natural kinds and famous people, "butterflies" would yield the answer "Nabokov" as surely as "hemlock" would trigger "Socrates." . . . After all, Humbert pursued nymphets, not Nymphalids, Luzhin captured chessmen, not Checkerspots, Pnin accumulated sorrows, not Sulphurs. Why did butterflies so fascinate Nabokov, and why should that so fascinate us?

In his introduction to *Nabokov's Butterflies: Unpublished and Uncollected Writings*, literary biographer Brian Boyd begins with a quotation from Nabokov—"My pleasures are the most intense known to man: writing and butterfly hunting"—to justify his own appropriation of butterflies as an extended metaphor for Nabokov's gorgeous, fluttering prose:

Let me pin Vladimir Nabokov into place alongside several superficially similar specimens.

From this point on, literature and Lepidoptera dance an elaborate pas de deux through seventy years of Nabokov's life.

Whenever a butterfly or moth plucked from its natural habitat in a particular novel demands attention, identification, and explanation, the anthologist's net suddenly becomes the reader's lens.

Boyd notes that "from as far back as we can see, Nabokov had a love of both detail and design, of precise, unpredictable particulars and intricate, often concealed patterns." One might say the same of Boyd, whose carefully constructed displays match Nabokov's in their stylistic virtuosity. In addition to metaphor, Boyd deploys alliteration and wordplay ("nymphets, not Nymphalids"; "chessmen, not Checkerspots"), active verbs *(yield, trigger, pursue, capture, accumulate, fascinate, pin, dance, pluck)*, and concrete details (butterfly names, literary characters, specimen boards, nets, lenses, ballet steps) to communicate the vibrancy and variety of Nabokov's prose.

milk production with the words "Consider a spherical cow in a vacuum."[6]

Figurative devices such as *simile, metaphor,* and *personification* show and tell in a different way, weaving memorable imagery into the very fabric of a writer's sentences. Some academics, particularly scientists and social scientists, regard figurative language with suspicion, associating metaphor and its cousins with the flowery, emotive outpourings of the novelist or poet. Yet scientists frequently invoke physical metaphors—Petri nets (computer science), DNA bar codes (molecular biology), step-down therapy (medicine)—to explain the work they do. Indeed, philosophers of language George Lakoff and Mark Johnson have argued that *all* language is deeply metaphorical; the language of embodied experience, they claim, is (metaphorically) hardwired into our very brains.[7]

Stylish academic writers choose their metaphors carefully, harnessing the physical world in the service of abstract ideas, as when literary theorist Peter Brooks and psychologist Robert J. Sternberg ascribe physical qualities to *argument* and *intimacy,* respectively:

> The plot of my own argument in this study will make loops and detours in the pursuit of its subject.[8]
> The swinging back and forth of the intimacy pendulum provides some of the excitement that keeps many relationships alive.[9]

Sometimes, however, academic writers let their metaphors choose them:

> In this chapter I have tracked rhetorical paths of thought to illustrate some ways rhetorical hermeneutics works as theory and as critical practice. Following these paths reveals how interpretations of phronesis have historically tied rhetoric and hermeneutics together.[10]

Here, literary theorist Steven Mailloux's ambition to "track rhetorical paths of thought" is derailed by conflicting metaphors—

illustrate, tie together, tool—that get in the way of his dominant "tracking" image. A writer more attentive to the workings of figurative language would stick to the *path* alone.

When an author strings several related comparisons together—"as A is like B, so C is like D"—we move into the realm of *analogy,* or extended metaphor. Scientists frequently use analogies to explain the workings of nature and the unseen world. In 1940, for example, biologist H. B. Cott noted that interdependent species engage in mutually escalating evolutionary behaviors:

> The fact is, that in the primeval struggle of the jungle, as in the refinements of civilized warfare, we see in progress a great evolutionary armament race. . . . Just as greater speed in the pursued has developed in relation to increased speed in the pursuer; or defensive armour in relation to aggressive weapons; so the perfection of concealing devices has evolved in response to increased powers of perception.[11]

Cott's "evolutionary arms race" analogy—animal species are like nations at war, heightened perception is like a weapon, camouflaging devices are like defensive armor—has been taken up and elaborated upon by numerous other scientists, including biologist Leigh Van Valen, who in 1972 coined the phrase "Red Queen's hypothesis" to explain how evolutionary systems maintain their fitness relative to other codeveloping systems. Van Valen's theory takes its name from the scene in Lewis Carroll's *Through the Looking Glass* where the Red Queen tells Alice that she must run faster and faster just to stay in the same square of the chessboard: "It takes all the running you can do, to keep in the same place."[12] Both Cott's evolutionary arms race and Van Valen's Red Queen's hypothesis belong to a long list of analogies that scientists and scholars have drawn upon to help us make sense of our world. Computer programmers "boot" their hard drives (the term derives from the phrase "pulling yourself up by your bootstraps"), linguists who study metaphor and analogy speak of "conceptual mappings," and educators construct pedagogical "scaffolding" to help their students learn. Sometimes such analogies can be misleading; for example, so-called "junk DNA," which denotes noncoding portions of a genome sequence, has turned out to have more important biological functions than its throwaway name would suggest.[13] Many scientific analogies, however, are so effective and compelling that they have entered our cultural lexicon and perhaps our very consciousness. The programmer who first slapped familiar office labels onto various computer functions—"desktop," "file," "folder," "control panel," "recycle bin"—certainly knew something about human psychology and our hunger for language that invokes physical reality.

Van Valen's Red Queen analogy is also an *allusion,* a device used by stylish authors such as anthropologist Ruth Behar and literary scholar Marjorie Garber to link abstract concepts with stories and images already familiar to most readers:

> To write vulnerably is to open a *Pandora's box.* Who can say what will come flying out?[14]
>
> Assistant professors are shown this forking path: You cannot get there from here. Write a solid, scholarly book for specialists in your field; otherwise you will step off the *yellow brick road* to tenure.[15]

We know that Pandora's box contains unknown dangers and that the yellow brick road leads to a place of Technicolor happiness—unless, of course, we are unfamiliar with Greek mythology and *The Wizard of Oz,* in which case the allusions fall flat. (Garber's passage also contains a veiled allusion to Jorge Luis Borges's short story "The Garden of the Forking Paths.") A careful stylist will either provide an explicit reference to the source being cited (as Van Valen does with his Red Queen's hypothesis) or, as in the two examples above, he or she will ensure that a sentence still makes sense even if a reader does not "get" the allusion.

STEVEN PINKER

This book tries to illuminate the nature of language and mind by choosing a single phenomenon and examining it from every angle imaginable. That phenomenon is regular and irregular verbs, the bane of every language student. At first glance that approach might seem to lie in the great academic tradition of knowing more and more about less and less until you know everything about nothing. But please don't put the book down just yet. Seeing the world in a grain of sand is often the way of science, as when geneticists agreed to study the lowly fruit fly so that their findings might cumulate into a deep understanding that would have been impossible had each scientist started from scratch with a different organism. Like fruit flies, regular and irregular verbs are small and easy to breed.

Psycholinguist Steven Pinker opens his book *Words and Rules: The Ingredients of Language* with a concrete, easy-to-grasp explanation of his methodology: he seeks to "illuminate the nature of language and mind" (a lofty ambition indeed) by focusing on a single grammatical exemplar, the irregular verb. His opening passage draws on just about every technique in the stylish writer's tool kit:

- a clearly stated thesis ("This book tries to illuminate")
- vivid verbs *(illuminate, choose, examine, cumulate, breed)*
- colorful nouns and adjectives *(bane, from scratch, lowly)*
- direct conversation with the reader ("But please")
- self-deprecating humor ("the great academic tradition of knowing more and more about less and less")
- literary allusions ("To see the world in a grain of sand"—William Blake)
- metaphor and analogy ("Like fruit flies, regular and irregular verbs are small and easy to breed")

Even Pinker's chapter titles—"Broken Telephone," "The Horrors of the German Language," "A Digital Mind in an Analog World"—are by turn concrete, humorous, allusive, and thought-provoking. Nearly every paragraph of his book contains examples, illustrations, or other manifestations of the "show and tell" principle at work.

Examples, metaphors, and allusions work their magic by painting pictures in our minds: we can practically see those hapless young assistant professors setting out merrily along the yellow brick road to tenure, still unaware of the hazards (lions and tigers and bears!) that lurk in the bushes along the way. *Visual illustrations,* by contrast—photos, drawings, diagrams, graphs—literally show us in images what the author tells in words. As neuropsychologist Allan Paivio and others have documented, words and images are processed by the brain along entirely separate pathways; unsurprisingly, readers understand new concepts more clearly and recall them more readily when they are presented both verbally and visually rather than just one way or the other.[16] The most effective illustrations, by and large, are those that complement rather than duplicate the text: a well-chosen diagram, graph, or screen shot speaks mostly for itself without requiring a long-winded explanation. At the same time, authors do no one a favor by dropping in illustrations that never get mentioned in the text. Nor do confusing or badly constructed graphics serve the stylish academic writer's cause. Convoluted flow charts and snazzy 3-D bar graphs can end up alienating rather than enlightening readers, who expect illustrations to forge an uncluttered path to the ideas and data presented in the text, not to throw up new roadblocks (see Figure 9.1).

The "show and tell" principle can be adapted to suit any academic context or disciplinary style. At the sentence level, a single concrete verb—*sweep, illuminate, forge*—helps lift a phrase into the realm of lived experience. Metaphors and analogies produce a similar effect, but more explicitly and on a more expansive scale. Anecdotes, case studies, and scenarios add narrative energy and human interest. Visual illustrations activate the eyes as well as the mind. Each of these techniques relies on a breathtakingly simple formula: abstract concepts become more memorable and accessible the moment we ground them in the material world, the world that our readers can see and touch.

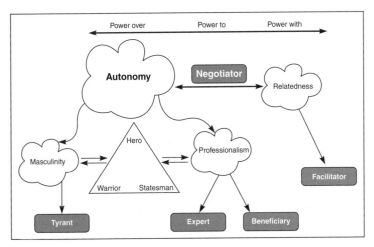

Figure 9.1. Example of a higher education diagram that risks confusing rather than enlightening readers with its various labels, arrows, and clouds. The caption to the original diagram reads, "Leadership discourses, subject positions, and corresponding modalities of power."

THINGS TO TRY

- *Examples:* For every sentence that you write about an abstract concept or principle, follow up with the words "For example . . ." This technique can lead to stylistic monotony if overused; however, if you are stuck for ideas, it is a good way to get you started thinking concretely. (Rule of thumb: Use the phrase "for example" no more than once per paragraph or, better yet, once per page. Cultivate other, more subtle ways to introduce examples.)
- *Anecdotes:* Start a file of anecdotes—ministories no more than a few sentences or paragraphs long—that relate to your research area. Weave them into your research writing at key points, whether to assist your readers' understanding or simply to regain their attention. If you don't know

where to start, try using an anecdote as your opening hook.

- *Case Studies:* If your research involves human subjects, consider framing it as a case study: that is, an exemplary story (see Chapter 8, "The Story Net," for further examples and ideas).

- *Scenarios:* A scenario presents a hypothetical situation and explores its possible outcomes. As a prompt, start by addressing your reader directly with an imperative verb such as *imagine, picture,* or *suppose.* You can later remove this direct address and present the scenario on its own.

- *Figurative Language:* Stylish writers employ similes, metaphors, analogies, and other figurative language to capture their readers' attention, aid their understanding, appeal to their physical senses, and generate new ideas. If figurative language doesn't come naturally to you, try the following steps:

  - Choose a bland, abstract sentence from your book, thesis, or article. (Example: "Speech errors occur frequently in human conversation, but the many different varieties of errors have not yet been adequately analyzed and categorized by scholars.")
  - Identify the subject of the sentence and come up with some concrete similes. ("Speech errors are like: sprouting weeds, lost children, swarming insects.")
  - Choose one of those similes and expand it into an analogy. ("If speech errors are like swarming insects, then the people who study them are like entomologists, and the act of studying them is like catching and classifying insects.")
  - Get playful with the analogy: push its limits, explore its shadow side. ("If speech errors are like swarming insects, studying them is like intentionally walking into a cloud of mosquitoes. If linguists are like entomologists, classifying speech errors is like dipping butterflies in formaldehyde and pinning them to a board.")

- Now work the analogy into your original sentence, as linguists Douglas Hofstadter and David Moser do when they invoke the "speech errors are like insects" analogy in a statement about error making and human cognition: "Speech errors of all kinds swarm in our linguistic environment like hordes of variegated insects waiting to be caught, labeled, and categorized."[17]
- Finally, try out your metaphorically enriched writing on a few colleagues—the conservative ones as well as those who are stylistically adventurous. Do they like it? Do you?

- *Visual illustrations* can be inviting, distracting, confusing, or illuminating, depending on how they are used. As with any other aspect of stylish writing, the key principle is to employ them self-consciously and with a clear sense of purpose:

  - For each illustration you include, ask yourself, "Why do I need this image? How does it aid the reader's understanding? Does my illustration supplement rather than duplicate what is already in the text?"
  - Because images are relatively expensive to print but easy to reproduce digitally, add colorful illustrations to Web-based publications and live presentations (subject to copyright provisions, of course) but use them sparingly in print.

CHAPTER 10

JARGONITIS

Every discipline has its own specialized language, its membership rites, its secret handshake. I remember the moment when, as a PhD student in comparative literature, I casually dropped the phrase "psychosexual morphology" into a discussion of a Thomas Hardy novel. What power! From the professor's approving nod and the envious shuffling of my fellow students around the seminar table, I knew that I had just flashed the golden badge that admitted me into an elite disciplinary community. Needless to say, my new party trick fell flat on my nonacademic friends and relations. Whenever I solemnly intoned the word "Foucauldian," they quickly went off to find another beer.

In its most benign and neutral definition, *jargon* signifies "the technical terminology or characteristic idiom of a special activity or group." More often, however, the jingly word that Chaucer used to describe "the inarticulate utterance of birds" takes on a pejorative cast: "unintelligible or meaningless talk or writing"; "nonsense, gibberish"; "a strange, outlandish, or barbarous language or dialect"; "obscure and often pretentious language marked by circumlocutions and long words."[1] So when does technical terminology cross over into the realm of *outlandish, obscure,* and *pretentious?* And how can academics communicate effectively with one another without exposing themselves to the contempt, derision, or irritation of those who do not understand them?

Many thoughtful and eloquent academics have defended the use of jargon in appropriate contexts. Derek Attridge observes that jargon makes transparent what other modes of critical discourse seek to hide, namely, the contingent and contextualized nature of language itself.[2] Roland Barthes describes jargon as "a way of imagining" that "shocks as imagination does."[3] Jacques Derrida, whose exuberantly neologistic prose has charmed and exasperated several generations of humanities scholars, dwells on the material pleasures of difficult language, noting that words like *jargon* and its cousin *argot* are chokingly ugly yet bizarrely sensual: "They both come from the bottom of the throat, they linger, for a certain time, like a gargling, at the bottom of the gullet, you rasp and you spit" ("Ils sortent tous deux du fond de la gorge, ils séjournent, un certain temps, comme un gargarisme, au fond du gosier, on racle et on crache").[4] What these commentators have in common is a deep respect for language that engages and challenges. None of them advocates lazy or pretentious writing—which, all too often, is what disciplinary jargonizing amounts to.

In his classic 1946 essay "Politics and the English Language," George Orwell demonstrates how any writer can turn powerful prose into mushy pablum—"modern English of the worst sort"—by replacing evocative nouns and resonant cadences with impersonal, abstract terminology:

> I returned and saw under the sun, that the race is not to the swift, nor the battle to the strong, neither yet bread to the wise, nor yet riches to men of understanding, nor yet favour to men of skill; but time and chance happeneth to them all. (Ecclesiastes 9:11)
>
> Objective considerations of contemporary phenomena compel the conclusion that success or failure in competitive activities exhibits no tendency to be commensurate with innate capacity, but that a considerable element of the unpredictable must invariably be taken into account. (Orwell's translation into standard bureaucrat-speak)[5]

MARJORIE GARBER

Shibboleth thus came to mean a word used as a test for detecting foreigners and also, by extension, a catchword used by a party or sect to identify members and exclude outsiders. In this sense academic jargon itself functions as a kind of shibboleth. . . . Jargon is any kind of language that has been overused and now substitutes for thought, a mere container for thinking, a verbal gesture rather than an idea, whether highly technical or highly banal. . . . Jargon marks the place where thinking has been. It becomes a kind of macro, to use a computer term: a way of storing a complicated sequence of thinking operations under a unique name.

In *Academic Instincts,* a study of academic versus journalistic discourse, literary critic and cultural theorist Marjorie Garber offers a nuanced and largely sympathetic analysis of scholarly jargon. She echoes Aristotle's advice that poets should not balk from using "unusual words" and notes that "a difficult text may be worth the trouble of deciphering." For her, the question at stake is not how to avoid jargon altogether, but "how to keep language at once precise and rich."

Garber's discussion of jargon models the judicious use of jargon. Describing jargon as a *shibboleth,* she defines a resonant historical term even while appropriating it for her own purposes: any reader previously unfamiliar with the concept has just acquired a new vocabulary word, a new nugget of knowledge, as well as a new way of understanding the cultural complexities of jargon. Next, she uses concrete images *(container, gesture)* to explain the abstract workings of jargon. Finally, she offers a compelling metaphor ("jargon is like a computer macro") that carefully incorporates a clear, precise definition of the specialist word *macro.* Her language is indeed "at once precise and rich," studded with anecdotes, allusions, examples, quotations, figurative language, and subtle humor.

The annals of academe are filled with examples of hoaxes based on parodies of scholarly discourse, from the fake "Spectrism" poetry movement of the 1920s to the infamous Sokal Affair of the 1990s, which reached its apogee when physicist Alan Sokal successfully placed "an article liberally salted with nonsense" in the cultural studies journal *Social Text* and then publically boasted about his feat.[6] As Sokal demonstrated, a satirist with a finely tuned ear can simulate the signature style of just about any academic discipline. So, indeed, can a cleverly programmed computer. The following passages were automatically generated by online "chatterbots" designed to parrot the prose of postmodernists, computer scientists, and the linguist Noam Chomsky, respectively:

> The main theme of von Ludwig's analysis of postsemioticist rationalism is a mythopoetical totality.
>
> After years of theoretical research into flip-flop gates, we prove the analysis of massive multiplayer online role-playing games, which embodies the confirmed principles of fuzzy networking.
>
> Note that the speaker-hearer's linguistic intuition does not readily tolerate nondistinctness in the sense of distinctive feature theory.[7]

Based on fairly simple algorithms, each of these programs conjures up the kind of muddy, obscurantist prose that Orwell likened to the defensive response of "a cuttlefish spurting out ink."[8] But it is their heavy-handed jargon—*postsemioticist, mythopoetical, flip-flop gates, fuzzy networking, nondistinctness, feature theory*—that most clearly marks these sentences as "academic."

In my survey of one hundred recent writing guides, I found that twenty-one of the guides recommend against disciplinary jargon of any kind; forty-six caution that technical language should be used carefully, accurately, and sparingly; and thirty-three make no comment on the subject. I have yet to discover a single academic style guide that advocates a freewheeling embrace of jargon. Nevertheless, academic journals are awash in the stuff:

MIKE CRANG

The centrality of visual depiction to student imaginations of geography was brought home to me when some years ago—presumably, back then, as a symbol of a "youthful" department—I was posed for a photo intended for use in the prospectus, lecturing a class that had been helpfully herded from the back of the hall to fill the front rows. The photographer positioned me standing behind the vast laboratory desk, while they provided a wall map of—I think I recall—Latin America, and to finalise the piece requested that I fast-forward to my most colourful slide to have it projected behind me. So in order to symbolise the classroom experience, we had audience, authoritative lectern, map—and, yes, slide. This, then, was geography as 17-year-olds would grasp it.

In an article memorably titled "The Hair in the Gate: Visuality and Geographical Knowledge," geographer Mike Crang offers a highly visual anecdote to illustrate the importance of visual symbols in the geography classroom. The abstract concepts around which his article revolves—"visuality and geographical knowledge"—are brought to life through concrete details: the photographer, the prospectus, the students "helpfully herded" to the front rows of the lecture, the "vast laboratory desk," the wall map of Latin America, the colorful slide.

In the very next paragraph, Crang shifts into standard academese:

An examination of this constellation of representation, power and knowledge seems all the more imperative as the rising hegemony (and, I am tempted to say, epistemological monopoly) of Microsoft's PowerPoint reinforces the interchangeability of content within the single (re)presentational system.

This is a monstrous sentence, filled with weighty abstractions—"constellation of representation," "rising hegemony," "epistemological monopoly," "(re)presentational system"—leavened by just one proper noun ("Microsoft's PowerPoint"). Yet Crang gets away with it because his descent into jargon is brief, lively ("I am tempted to say"), and to the point. Within another sentence or two, his prose is back on track again: vigorous, varied, and concrete.

Tomita extended LR parsing, not by backtracking and lookahead but by a breadth-first simulation of multiple LR parsers spawned by nondeterminism in the LR table. [Computer Science]

Moreover, central aspects of Holland's theory are structurally represented in the RIASEC interest circumplex wherein an explicit set of relations between variables in the interest domain are specified. [Psychology]

By bringing deconstructive techniques to political philosophy, a theoretical discourse of rationality and self-control is forced to come to terms with the metaphorical, catachrestical, and fabulistic materials buried within it. [Literary Studies]

These extracts all appeared in articles with "jargonicity ratios" of 1:10 or higher; that is, their authors employ specialized terminology on average once in every ten words, if not more. Only the first example, a vigorously phrased if otherwise incomprehensible sentence from a computer science article, stands up to syntactical scrutiny. In the other two sentences, jawbreakers such as *circumplex* and *catachrestical* momentarily distract us from serious grammatical errors: in the psychology article, a singular noun *(set)* is modified by a plural verb *(are),* while the literary studies extract opens with a dangling participle *(by bringing*—who brings?) and closes with an ambiguous *it* (*philosophy* or *discourse?*). If the authors of these sentences are so intoxicated by big words that they cannot keep their own syntax walking in a straight line, what chance do their readers have?

In many academic contexts, jargon functions as a highly efficient form of disciplinary shorthand: phrases such as "non-HACEK gram-negative bacillus endocarditis" (medicine) or "unbounded demonic and angelic nondeterminacy" (computer science) may be unintelligible to ordinary mortals, but they facilitate efficient communication among disciplinary experts (or so I am assured by the latter). Sometimes, however, the line between technical precision and intellectual pretension becomes a fine one. Take, for example, the word *Foucauldian,* which I employed satirically at the beginning of this chapter as an example of potentially off-putting jargon. In my one thousand–article data sample, I found eighteen articles from humanities and social science journals that mention the cultural theorist Michel Foucault at least once within their first few pages. Seven of these articles contain the F-word in its adjectival form, variously invoking: from higher education, "Foucauldian theory," "a Foucauldian analysis of power," and "the Foucauldian interplay between 'constraint' and 'agency' "; from literary studies, "a Foucauldian understanding of the operations of power and the repressive hypothesis" and "Foucauldian assumptions about genre as an agentless discourse"; and from history, "the Foucauldian concept of 'discourse' " and a "Foucauldian direction" of thought. Four of the articles lay claim to Foucauldian ideas, while the other three challenge Foucauldian paradigms. Only two of the seven articles, however, actually engage with Foucault's work in any meaningful way: in one, the authors claim that "Foucauldian theory lays the groundwork for the methodological approach used in this investigation," but it turns out that their understanding of "Foucauldian theory" has been gleaned almost entirely from a 1994 book on Foucault and feminism; in the other, the authors repeatedly refer to Foucault's work on imperialist discourse, but only as refracted through the writings of Edward Said. None of the seven articles provides evidence that its authors have actually read and engaged with Foucault's work themselves. Far from being wielded by these scholars as a precision instrument to facilitate a nuanced understanding among experts, the word "Foucauldian" becomes a sort of semantic shotgun, scattering meaning in all directions.

Stylish academic writers do not deny the utility of jargon, nor do they eschew its intellectual and aesthetic pleasures. Instead, they deploy specialized language gracefully, cautiously, and meticulously, taking care to keep their readers on board. For example, when educational researchers Ray Land and Siân Bayne appropriate the Foucauldian term *panopticon* in a discussion of disciplinary surveillance in online learning environments, they provide a succinct historical overview of the concept, grounded in

MICHEL FOUCAULT

In order to be exercised, this power had to be given the instrument of permanent, exhaustive, omnipresent surveillance, capable of making all visible, as long as it could itself remain invisible. It had to be like a faceless gaze that transformed the whole social body into a field of perception: thousands of eyes posted everywhere, mobile attentions ever on the alert, a long, hierarchized network which, according to Le Maire, comprised for Paris the forty-eight commissaires, the twenty inspecteurs, then the "observers," who were paid regularly, the "basses mouches," or secret agents, who were paid by the day, then the informers, paid according to the job done, and finally the prostitutes. And this unceasing observation had to be accumulated in a series of reports and registers; throughout the eighteenth century, an immense police text increasingly covered society by means of a complex documentary organization.

Where have all those self-proclaimed Foucauldians picked up their love of jargon? Certainly not from Foucault himself, whose influential writings on discipline, power, sexuality, and other weighty matters are rhythmically compelling, relentlessly concrete, and almost entirely jargon-free.

In this passage, Foucault analyzes an abstract concept, *power*, via the physical trope of *surveillance*, which he animates with three perfectly pitched adjectives *(permanent, exhaustive, omnipresent)* and a spooky corporeal metaphor *(faceless gaze, social body, thousands of eyes)* before going on to document the long reach of various surveillance instruments into the lives of real people (commissaries, inspectors, observers, secret agents, informers, prostitutes) in a specific time and place (eighteenth-century Paris). Like many writers alert to stylistic nuance, Foucault alternates long sentences with short ones, building and maintaining a dynamic rhythmic flow. He tells stories: his book *Discipline and Punish*, for example, opens with a harrowing account of a criminal being drawn and quartered, an image that sticks in the reader's mind long afterward. He weaves one concrete example after another into his densely analytical but richly textured prose. And he quotes from primary sources only if he has actually read them himself.

Foucault's own writings.[9] When literary critic Peter Brooks imports the Russian formalist terms *fabula* and *sjužet* into his book *Reading for the Plot,* he deftly glosses both terms and explains how they contribute to a deeper understanding of stories and plots.[10] When philosopher Jacques Derrida coins a new word, *différance,* to signify semantic differences that lead to an endless deferral of meaning, he explains at length the thinking behind his neologism.[11] These authors hand their readers complex tools—but always with instructions attached.

Academics turn to jargon for a wide variety of reasons: to display their erudition, to signal membership in a disciplinary community, to demonstrate their mastery of complex concepts, to cut briskly into an ongoing scholarly conversation, to push knowledge in new directions, to challenge readers' thinking, to convey ideas and facts efficiently, and to play around with language. Many of these motivations align well with the ideals of stylish academic writing. Wherever jargon shows its shiny face, however, the demon of academic hubris inevitably lurks in the shadows nearby. Academics who are committed to using language effectively and ethically—as a tool for communication, not as an emblem of power—need first of all to acknowledge the seductive power of jargon to bamboozle, obfuscate, and impress.

THINGS TO TRY

- If you suspect that you suffer from jargonitis, start by measuring the scope of your addiction. Print out a sample of your academic writing and highlight *every word* that would not be immediately comprehensible to a reader from outside your own discipline. (Alternatively, you can ask such a reader to do the highlighting for you.) Do you use jargon more than once per page, per paragraph, per sentence?
- Next, ask yourself some hard questions about your motivations. Do you employ jargon to:

- impress other people?
- signal your membership in a disciplinary community?
- demonstrate your mastery of complex ideas?
- enter an academic conversation that is already under way?
- play with language and ideas?
- create new knowledge?
- challenge your readers' thinking?
- communicate succinctly with colleagues?

Retain only those jargon words that clearly serve your priorities and values.
- For every piece of jargon that you decide to keep, make sure you give your readers a secure handhold: a definition, some background information, a contextualizing word or phrase. By the time you have clarified your usage, you might even find that you can let go of the word itself.

STRUCTURAL DESIGNS

Essayist Annie Dillard describes writing as an architectural endeavor, a continuous cycle of design, demolition, and rebuilding. Sentences are the bricks; paragraphs are the walls and windows:

> Some of the walls are bearing walls; they have to stay, or everything will fall down. Other walls can go with impunity. . . . Unfortunately, it is often a bearing wall that has to go. It cannot be helped. There is only one solution, which appalls you, but there it is. Knock it out. Duck.[1]

Dillard's metaphor strikes at the emotional heart of the writing process, which involves destruction as well as production, short-term losses as well as long-term gains. Stylish academic writers are craftspeople who regard their texts as intricate, labor-intensive structures that must be carefully planned and meticulously built, from the pouring of the foundation and the sourcing of the materials to the final polishing of the banisters—not to mention those rare but wrenching occasions when the wrecking ball must be called in.

A well-structured article or book, like a well-built house, requires careful thought and planning. Most academics enjoy a wider range of structural choices than they may realize, starting with the most basic decision of all: will their overall structure be conventional, unique, or something in between? As a general rule, disciplinary cultures that value creative expression (such as literary studies) encourage and reward creatively structured scholarship, whereas disciplinary cultures that privilege scientific rigor (such as biology) encourage and reward structural rigor. However, of the ten disciplines in my data sample, medicine was the only field in which 100 percent of the articles employed a conventional Introduction, Method, Results, and Discussion (IMRAD) structure or something very similar, with absolutely no variations. In every other discipline surveyed, I observed a range of structural approaches. Significant percentages of academics in computer science (90 percent), higher education (70 percent), psychology (56 percent), anthropology (50 percent), and even evolutionary biology (10 percent) adopted unique or hybrid rather than purely conventional structures. In the humanities, meanwhile, I noted a fairly even mix of articles with unique structures (that is, their section titles follow no recognizable pattern or convention), hybrid structures (whereby uniquely titled sections cohabit with conventionally titled sections), and sequential structures (sections that are numbered but not titled). More than one-third of the history and literature articles in my survey sample—36 percent and 38 percent, respectively—contained no section headings at all (see Figure 2.1 in Chapter 2).

For scientists and social scientists, the advantages of adhering to a conventional structure are many. Authors who follow the IMRAD model always open their articles with an introductory section that clearly states the purpose and scope of the current research, sums up previous work in the field, and probes gaps and flaws in the existing literature. Next, in sections with titles such as "Data," "Methodology," and "Results" (the exact labels vary from field to field), they describe the data collection and results. Finally, in the "Analysis," "Discussion," and/or "Conclusion" sections, they review their main findings, explore the wider implications of their work, and offer suggestions for further research. This paint-by-numbers approach prompts researchers to plan their research methodically, conduct it rigorously, and present it

DONALD SHANKWEILER

At the beginning of our long collaboration, Isabelle Liberman and I were concerned with testing explanations of reading problems that were current at the end of the 1960s. At that time, ideas about causation regularly invoked neuropsychological concepts such as poorly established cerebral dominance. Reversals of letters and words were still considered to be the hallmark of dyslexia. . . . As for treatment, that was the heyday of motor patterning, balance beams, and eye exercises. Our early work was devoted more to showing what reading disability was not than to explaining what it was.

In an article that pays tribute to his recently deceased colleague Isabelle Liberman, linguist Donald Shankweiler explains how the concept of phonological awareness can help teachers help children with reading problems. Despite a plethora of *be* verbs and some sloppy locutions that demonstrate the pitfalls of abstraction (for example, "ideas about causation regularly invoked neuropsychological concepts"—can an idea invoke a concept?), Shankweiler's writing style is for the most part lucid, personable, and example-driven. He structures his article as a series of seven numbered assertions about "the development of reading and its difficulties," with each "assertion" constituting a section heading, for example:

1. Emergence of Phonological Awareness Follows a Developmental Pattern
2. Early Instruction Designed to Promote Phonological Awareness and Letter Knowledge Confers an Advantage in Reading and Spelling That Is Measurable Years Later

Readers come away from Shankweiler's article with a clear understanding of his seven arguments and of the evidence he musters to support each one. Rather than wrapping up with a standard conclusion, he ends with a "promissory note" that describes new research advances. Such news, he notes, would have given great pleasure to the friend and colleague whose work his article memorializes.

coherently, without leaving out any crucial information. More-over, a conventional structure is relatively easy for new academics to learn; all they have to do is follow models established by others before them. Readers, meanwhile, know exactly where to look for key findings. They can skim the abstract, mine the literature review, scan the data, and grab the conclusions without wasting valuable time actually *reading*.

However, conventional structures also have some significant drawbacks. Generic section titles such as "Method" and "Conclusion" provide very little real information about an article's content, a handicap for skimmers as well as for readers. In the following outline excerpted from a higher education journal, only the title tells us anything specific about the topic being addressed:

Title	Relationships among Structural Diversity, Informal Peer Interactions and Perceptions of the Campus Environment
Section Headings	Background
	Research Questions
	Research Method
	Conceptual Model
	Data Sources
	Measures
	Data Analysis
	Results

Another disadvantage of identically structured articles is that they all end up looking and sounding more or less alike, thus offering the subliminal impression that they all say more or less the same thing. Even more worryingly, academics who always plan, research, and write to a template risk thinking to a template as well.

Hybrid structures offer an alternative for scientists and social scientists who want to add some unique architectural features to work that is otherwise safely grounded in disciplinary norms. In a research article with a hybrid structure, sections with conventional titles such as "Introduction," "Method," or "Conclusion" sit side by side with uniquely titled sections such as "Gender and Developmental Issues Relative to Interest Structure" (psychology), "Pre-Classic Settlement, Ceramics, and Social Conflict in the Rio Grande del Rancho Drainage" (anthropology), or "Legalism in East Asian Regional Economic Integration" (law). The following outline of an article from a computer science journal offers a fairly typical example of a hybrid structure:

Title	Solving #SAT Using Vertex Covers
Section Titles	1. Introduction
	2. Sequential Recursive Petri Nets
	2.1 Definitions
	2.2 Expressivity of SRPNs
	2.3 Analysis of SRPNs
	3. Recursive Petri Nets
	3.1 Definitions
	3.2 An Illustrative Example
	3.3 Expressivity of RPNs
	3.4 Analysis of RPNs
	4. Conclusion

Note the parallel sequencing of the two main sections (Definitions, Expressivity, Analysis) and the numbered outline indicating structural hierarchies (a mandatory feature in many science and engineering journals). The authors of this article are not trying to impress anyone with their inventive structure and clever section titles. Nor, however, have they followed a predetermined template dictating how they must present their research.

Stylish academic writers often adapt conventional and hybrid structures to suit their own needs, as when psychologist Bob Altemeyer offers two brief Method-Results-Discussion studies within a single article, or when management researchers David Guest and Neil Conway set up a study based on five "Hypotheses," each of which is explained in the opening section, reported on in the "Results" section, and further analyzed in the

"Discussion" section.[2] Some authors use unique subsection headings to enliven and individualize conventionally titled main sections (a common ploy in evolutionary biology, among other fields). At the opposite end of the stylishness spectrum are articles so carelessly assembled that their structure exposes cracks and fissures in their authors' thinking. One of the higher education articles in my data sample, for instance, contains a section promisingly titled "Findings and Interpretations," which opens with the following sentence: "Four dominant discourses shaping images of leadership emerged from our analysis: *autonomy, relatedness, masculinity,* and *professionalism*" [my italics]. The reader therefore anticipates that the section will consist of four subsections arranged in the following sequence:

- Autonomy
- Relatedness
- Masculinity
- Professionalism

Instead, however, when we skim through the section, we discover that the authors have broken it into five subsections:

- Autonomy
- Gender and Masculinity
- Professionalism
- Masculinity
- Relatedness

Not only do the subsections occur in a different order than the opening sentence has led us to expect, but the "Masculinity" subsection has suddenly spawned a semi-redundant offshoot, "Gender and Masculinity." This lack of attention to structural detail—indeed, to structural fundamentals—leaves readers feeling rather as though we followed signs marked "Auditorium" and found ourselves in a broom closet. Worse, the structural inconsistencies make us doubt the validity of the authors' analysis; how could

ROBERT J. CONNORS AND ANDREA LUNSFORD

As we worked on this error research together, . . . we started somewhere along the line to feel less and less like the white-coated Researchers of our dreams and more and more like characters we called Ma and Pa Kettle— good-hearted bumblers striving to understand a world whose complexity was more than a little daunting. Being fans of classical rhetoric, *prosopopoeia, letteraturizzazione,* and the like, as well as enthusiasts for intertextuality, *plaisir de texte, différence,* etc., we offer this account of our travails.

In a now classic 1988 article titled "Frequency of Formal Errors in Current College Writing, or Ma and Pa Kettle Do Research," professors of composition Robert J. Connors and Andrea Lunsford report on a large-scale study of how composition instructors mark formal errors in student writing. Humorously describing their own awkward attempts to negotiate a research paradigm to which they brought plenty of naïve enthusiasm but no real disciplinary training or experience, they write with a stylistic audacity that matches their interdisciplinary chutzpah. Each section title pairs a weighty label drawn from classical rhetoric with a wry summary of "Ma and Pa Kettle's" shambolic progress:

- *Proem:* In Which the Characters Are Introduced
- *Exordium:* The Kettles Smell a Problem
- *Narratio:* Ma and Pa Visit the Library
- *Confirmatio I:* The Kettles Get Cracking
- *Confutatio:* Ma and Pa Suck Eggs
- *Confirmatio II:* Ma and Pa Hit the Road
- *Amplificatio:* Ma and Pa Hunker Down
- *Peroratio:* The Kettles Say, "Aw, Shucks"

Working collaboratively in a field where single authorship is a disciplinary norm, Connors and Lunsford push against every stylistic and structural boundary they can think of, playfully reflecting on both the processes and the products of their own research.

Figure 11.1. Virginia Woolf's sketch of the structure of *To the Lighthouse.*

such shoddy construction techniques possibly result in a water-tight building?

A seemingly unstructured but in fact well-crafted article provides a more satisfying reading experience—and certainly a more persuasive demonstration of authorial skill—than a conventionally structured one with weak supporting walls and confusing signposting. Virginia Woolf famously described her experimental 1927 novel *To the Lighthouse* as "two blocks joined by a corridor," sketching two large rectangles to represent the bulk of the novel, in which time moves very slowly, connected by a narrow band depicting the "Time Passes" section, in which years fly by in the blink of an eye (see Figure 11.1).[3]

As Woolf's example reminds us, structure becomes more rather than less important when an author deviates from generic norms and expectations. Unique and experimental structures can open up new ways of approaching familiar issues, a form of intellectual displacement that parallels the physical displacement we feel when we traverse an unfamiliar landscape or enter a room where the walls sit at unusual angles. Only if the route is well signposted and the rooms are well lit will readers be able to take such displacement in their stride.

In a conventionally structured academic article, section headings function like centrally positioned, neatly labeled doorways that lead us from one well-proportioned room to the next. In a uniquely structured article, by contrast, we never quite know where we are going or why, unless the author makes a special effort to keep us on track. In some humanities articles, the section headings feel more like partitions randomly inserted to break up a cavernous space than like the coherent components of an architectural plan:

Title	Godard Counts
Section Headings	1. Ordering Evidence
	2. Dirty Hands
	3. Counting on Your Fingers, Thinking with Your Hands
	4. The History of Oneself
	5. Public Aesthetics
	6. "Envoi 1"
	7. The Art of Living
	8. The Stakes of Style
	9. Perfectibility and Debasement

The author of this article from a prominent cultural studies journal, for example, has missed a golden opportunity to use his punning title as a structuring device: "Godard Counts" suggests not only that the filmmaker Jean-Luc Godard is important ("counts") but also that his aesthetics is bound up with tropes of numbering, ordering, and counting. The article's first three section titles ("Ordering Evidence," "Dirty Hands," "Counting on Your Fingers") echo the counting pun; but then the author drops the ball. The remaining six section titles have nothing much to do either with the main title or with one another, and the numbers impose a sequential flow that is not reflected in the titles. For a reader skimming the article in search of information and direction, the cryptic section titles prove more mystifying than helpful.

To be sure, not all humanities scholars want to provide their readers with clearly marked entry and exit points. Some compose playful section titles that mimic the brightly painted doors of a fun house, deliberately enticing us into halls of mirrors or other surprising spaces. Others eschew section titles altogether, calling on more subtle structuring techniques—the gradually unfolding argument, the controlling metaphor—to direct their readers' attention, as when literary scholar Linda Brodkey stitches together her childhood memories of reading, writing, and sewing in an article whose title, "Writing on the Bias," puns on the relationship between textile and text.[4] Peter Elbow's influential book *Writing with Power* contains many intriguing suggestions for variations on conventional structures (for example, the collage essay, the dialogic essay, or the critical-creative essay).[5] Elsewhere, in an essay titled "The Music of Form," Elbow notes that, while section headings help readers get a quick visual overview of an article, there is still something to be said for the linear, time-bound experience of moving through a piece of writing one word at a time:

> I'm not arguing against the usefulness of traditional organizational techniques like signposting, mapping, and thesis statements—which can powerfully compensate for how texts are trapped in the glue of time. But . . . the traditional techniques are not the only way to give readers a sense that an essay hangs together and is well organized.[6]

Authors of scholarly books—the mansions of academe—have the luxury of constructing architectural features that would not easily fit within the confined footprint of an individual research article: staircases and turrets, fountains and follies. Some build whole volumes around a unifying theme or metaphor, as when literary scholar Robert Pogue Harrison, in a book about forests in the Western literary imagination, invokes different forms and uses of forests in chapters with titles such as "Shadows of Law," "Forests of Nostalgia," "Dwelling," and "The Ecology of Finitude."[7] Some authors focus on the reader's journey, as when classicist David Ulansey structures his book on Mithraic religious rituals "as a gradual unveiling of a mystery . . . allowing the story to unfold step by step, slowly adding separate pieces to a puzzle whose final image does not become clear until the end."[8]

VICTORIA ROSNER

"Yes? No?" No. The opening lines of *Good Morning, Midnight* capture what seemed so wrong with the forms of private life in the first part of the twentieth century. Rootless and solitary, protagonist Sasha Jensen passes her time in a fruitless search for rooms. Rooms speak to her, tell her in suggestive tones what they're about. . . . Sasha warns the reader later of the latent power in the rooms she inspects: "Never tell the truth about this business of rooms, because it would bust the roof off everything and undermine the whole social system."

In a citation announcing the Modernist Studies Association's 2006 Book Prize for a "significant contribution to modernist studies," the selection committee drily noted, "It is a rare thing to be seduced by a table of contents." Victoria Rosner's multidisciplinary book *Modernism and the Architecture of Private Life* explores the domestic interiors of early twentieth-century art, literature, and thought by inviting us to wander through a series of beautifully composed chapters appropriately titled "Kitchen Table Modernism," "Frames," "Thresholds," "Studies," and "Interiors." Architecture provides Rosner not only with the structural design for her book but also with a treasure trove of evocative metaphors, from the literal "impasse" where novelist Jean Rhys's protagonist Sasha Jensen conducts her fruitless search for a room of her own—"a narrow alley that arcs and cuts off in a dead end"—to the complex web of relationships that shaped modernist culture:

This book proposes that the spaces of private life are a generative site for literary modernism. These spaces compose a kind of grid of social relations that shifts and slips, often upending the individuals who traverse it.

Rosner's highly spatial vocabulary—*space, site, grid, shift, slip, traverse*—illuminates abstract ideas about society and selfhood. Her book takes us from the laundry room to the library, from the closet to the study, and to many other places in between.

Some even set their readers loose in conceptual mazes deliberately designed to disorient and amuse, as when cognitive scientist and jack-of-all-disciplines Douglas Hofstadter, in books with titles like *I Am a Strange Loop* and *The Mind's I,* foregrounds the self-referential intricacies of his own writing.[9] Bold structural choices such as these are available not only to book authors but to dissertation writers as well, provided they have the necessary personal confidence and institutional support. As with any other aspect of academic writing, the key to producing a well-structured book, article, or thesis is neither slavish imitation nor willful anarchy but carefully considered craftsmanship.

THINGS TO TRY

- If you are a scientist or social scientist, decide in advance whether you want your journal article to have a conventional, hybrid, or unique structure. Pros and cons: a conventional IMRAD structure (Intro, Method, Results, and Discussion) encourages scientific rigor but discourages independent thinking; a unique structure promotes creativity but risks disorienting readers; a hybrid structure offers flexibility but is neither fish nor fowl.
- Consider using a metaphor, theme, or series of sequential steps as a structuring device.
- If you have never before strayed from IMRAD and its cousins, consider developing a hybrid structure or, at the very least, introducing some unique subsection titles. Look in journals from both within and beyond your discipline for examples.
- Make an outline of your article or book based *only* on its chapter titles or section headings. How well does that outline, on its own, communicate what your work is about? Are you using section headings to inform, engage, and direct your readers, or merely to carve up space?

- To fine-tune your structure, make a paragraph outline. First, identify the topic sentence of each paragraph (that is, the sentence that most clearly states its overall argument); next, arrange those sentences in a numbered sequence. This process can help you identify structural weaknesses both within and between paragraphs: for example, a paragraph that has no clearly stated argument or one that does not logically build on the one before.

CHAPTER 12

POINTS OF REFERENCE

What do citation styles have to do with stylishness? Everything. How we cite influences how we write, from the minutiae of bibliographic forms to the big picture of how we respond to and acknowledge other people's work. Academic authors do no favors to themselves or their readers if they neglect to give credit where credit is due. At the same time, however, a book or article weighed down by awkwardly placed parenthetical citations and ponderous footnotes will probably be less readable, less engaging, and ultimately less persuasive than a piece of writing that wears its scholarly apparatus lightly.

Many commentators have noted the powerful role of citation styles in reinforcing disciplinary epistemologies. All kinds of methodological prejudices lurk just below the surface of any academic text; when we disrupt normative elements such as citation styles, we send those unspoken assumptions scurrying out into the light. Frances Kelly, a literary scholar turned educational researcher, recalls the challenges she faced when she first had to write a paper using APA style (sanctioned by the American Psychological Association) rather than MLA style (sanctioned by the Modern Language Association):

> The first real difficulty arose when I attempted to discuss an article produced by a team of researchers working in collaboration. . . .

> Here is a sentence lifted from a draft of the first paper I wrote for a Higher Education conference: "Collins, Rendle-Short, Jowan, Curnow, and Liddicoat (2001) make a similar point to Morris in their call for a new postgraduate pedagogy that takes the broader picture into account (p. 123)." . . . What had been a conversational element of my writing style now seemed decidedly clumsy.[1]

Accustomed to citing authors' first names (which personalizes them), to knowing their gender (which contextualizes them), and to quoting their words directly (which privileges the opinions and experiences of individuals over disembodied assertions of fact), Kelly realized that she was trying to impose an "author prominent" way of thinking on a citation style that favors "information prominent" statements instead. Not only did she have to play down the role of academic authors as shapers of knowledge, but she also had to relinquish her habit of quoting the full titles of the books and articles she cited: "This was perhaps the most irksome of the changes I had to make to my writing because it struck at the very base of my disciplinary training and my sense of purpose (and even identity); if I wasn't discussing the texts, what was I doing?"

For some academics, the disciplinary assumptions imposed by particular citation styles are the whole point of the exercise. In an article aimed at teachers of undergraduate psychology courses, psychologists Robert Madigan, Susan Johnson, and Patricia Linton approvingly observe that APA style "encapsulates the core values and epistemology" of their discipline. Through mastery of the citational process, they argue, psychology students learn to recast a "complex human story" as a "sanitized, rationalized account of the research"; to challenge other researchers' findings by focusing on "empirical details rather than personalities"; to buffer their conclusions with hedging words such as *tend, suggest,* and *may;* to cite other authors by paraphrasing their arguments rather than quoting them directly; and to regard language not as a complex medium but as a "somewhat unimportant container for information about phenomena, data, and theories." Exposure to APA-style writing, the authors conclude, "can only help define for students the discipline of psychology and encourage the development of intellectual values that are typical of the discipline. A successful student comes not only to write like a psychologist but to think like one as well."[2]

Other scholars, however, offer a more cautious and critical view of the relationship between citation styles and intellectual empowerment. Rhetorician Robert J. Connors notes that parenthetical citation styles "relegate issues of readability and prose style to tertiary importance" and elevate "instruction" over "delight." Similarly, poet and literary critic Charles Bernstein warns that institutional prescriptions encourage authors to adopt a linear, univocal, straitjacketed prose style characterized by "frame lock, and its cousin tone jam."[3] Metaphors of containment, conformity, and even corsetry suffuse both authors' critiques: Connors documents how the rhetoric of citation systems has "silently undergirded the enterprise of Western intellectual activity," while Bernstein chastises the "generations of professional standard bearers and girdle makers" who inhibit originality by insisting on "appropriate scholarly decorum."[4]

Academic writers do indeed often chafe under the constriction of ill-fitting citation regimes; I remember my own frustration, years ago, at having to waste precious research time searching for an out-of-print edition of *The Chicago Manual of Style,* thanks to an obstinate editor who refused to update his journal's outmoded house style. However, I have never heard of an editor urging an author to add more and longer footnotes to an article or to cram yet another parenthetical citation into an already overloaded sentence. Although academics love to blame their own stylistic shortcomings on prescriptive gatekeepers, the responsibility for citing badly or well ultimately lies at their own front door. Even when authors cannot choose which citation style to use in a given publication, they can still choose *how* to use it.

PETER GOODRICH

In truth what we need, what is really missing, what science requires, what art desires but the law and economics types have overlooked, is a citation index exclusive to the asterisk footnote. It is here that you get the lowdown. These are the references that need to be counted, ranked, listed, and tabulated. These are the veridical marks of community, the unexpurgated indicia of affiliations, the slips that signal the form of life, the motive and the militating purpose. [Excerpt from footnote]

Legal scholar Peter Goodrich takes satirical footnotes to a whole new level when, in the first of the 601 footnotes annotating his article "Satirical Legal Studies," he calls for a more rigorous referencing of references. Like any good satirist, Goodrich mixes humor with serious critique. With his insistently repeated *what*s ("In truth *what* we need, *what* is really missing, *what* science requires, *what* art desires"), his conspiratorial asides ("It is here that you get the lowdown"), his intentionally redundant vocabulary ("counted, ranked, listed, and tabulated"), and his over-the-top turns of phrase ("the veridical marks of community, the unexpurgated indicia of affiliations, the slips that signal the form of life"), he mocks not only the pedantry of the legal scholar but also the inflated rhetoric of the courtroom lawyer.

In his article, Goodrich catalogs numerous examples of legal satire, including a law review article in which the main text "literally falls into a footnote" and many other "gems . . . buried in the interstices of articles on the most somber of substantive doctrines." His 120-page article not only demonstrates his own mastery of the legal satire genre but, even more impressively, documents his nuanced understanding of the litigational and scholarly paradigms within which he and his colleagues operate.

In this book, in keeping with my publisher's preferences, I employ "*Chicago* style" endnotes, following the format specified in *The Chicago Manual of Style*. As an interdisciplinary scholar who also frequently works with the MLA and APA styles, I am well acquainted with both the pros and cons of the *Chicago* style, which consigns all bibliographic material to endnotes indicated in the main text by superscript numerals. On the plus side, *Chicago* endnotes are logical and compact; they sweep the text free of parenthetical obstructions and negate the need for a separate "Works Cited" section, as all of the relevant bibliographic information appears in the notes themselves. Whereas footnotes disrupt the flow of the text by drawing our eyes to the bottom of each page, endnotes remain discreetly discrete: readers do not have to consult them unless they want to. On the minus side, those ubiquitous little note numbers can function, in the words of architectural historian Lewis Mumford, like "barbed wire" maintaining a spiky distance between the readers and the text.[5] In a book intended to reach a wide range of readers, endnotes and footnotes alike risk communicating at best a scholarly pretentiousness—"Let me show you how erudite I am"—and at worst a sort of fussy didacticism: "This text is far too difficult for you to understand on your own; please allow me to explain it to you."

Long discursive annotations, in particular, can hamper the narrative flow of an academic text, luring readers down distracting side paths when the author's main job is to get them from A to B. Not all academics would agree, however, that discursive notes are best avoided even in scholarly prose intended for specialist readers. Laurel Richardson lauds discursive notes as "a place for secondary arguments, novel conjectures, and related ideas"; Robert J. Connors calls them the "alleys, closes and mews" where authors abandon the "high street of the text" to pursue subversive arguments and analysis.[6] These divergent opinions serve as a salient reminder that stylishness remains, in the end, a matter of personal taste: one reader's poison may turn out to be another's cup of tea.

Indeed, for many academics, footnotes and endnotes offer an unmowed corner of grass where they can let their proverbial hair down and run wild. Vladimir Nabokov exploited the satirical promise of the scholarly endnote in his novel *Pale Fire,* ostensibly an annotated edition of a long poem by the fictional poet John Shade, but in fact an autobiography cum murder mystery whose elaborate, paranoiac plot snakes through the voluminous notes allegedly penned by Charles Kinbote (also known as King Charles of Zembla), a former neighbor of the dead poet.[7] Following Nabokov's example, stylish authors such as psychologist Michael Corballis and philosopher Ted Cohen have published academic books and articles that contain irreverent notes among the serious ones:

> It appears that bats do not intentionally signal the presence of prey to other bats but simply adventitiously pick up echolocation signals from them. This rather suggests that bats do not possess theory of mind. I'm sorry you had to wait this long to learn about bats.[8]
>
> My appreciation of *Chinatown,* and of many other things, owes much to Joel Snyder, one of the world's best conversational colleagues. It is difficult to find—and luck to have found—a friend who is very intelligent, highly critical, and also endlessly sympathetic. If the characters in *Chinatown* had friends like that, the movie would have a happy ending, and it would be a failure.[9]

Legal journals, in which footnotes frequently climb halfway up the pages or higher, provide a particularly fertile ground for satirists, including a law professor whose article on "Satirical Legal Studies" contains 601 footnotes (see "Spotlight on Style: Peter Goodrich") and a group of law students whose tongue-in-cheek article on "The Common Law Origins of the Infield Fly Rule" footnotes the opening word "The."[10]

In an absorbing book-length study of the footnote, historian Tony Grafton observes that footnotes "flourished most brightly in the eighteenth century, when they served to comment ironically on the narrative in the text as well as to support its veracity."

ANTHONY GRAFTON

Like the high whine of the dentist's drill, the low rumble of the footnote on the historian's page reassures: the tedium it inflicts, like the pain inflicted by the drill, is not random but directed, part of the cost that the benefits of modern science and technology exact. . . . Historians for whom composing annotations has become second nature—like dentists who have become inured to inflicting pain and shedding blood—may hardly notice any more that they still extrude names of authors, titles of books, and numbers of folders in archives or leaves in unpublished manuscripts.

Historian Tony Grafton brings a stylish blend of erudition and humor to every topic he addresses, no matter how seemingly trivial or banal. In his book *The Footnote: A Curious History*, he provides numerous examples—some serious, some silly—of how scholars' arguments "stride forward or totter backward" on their footnotes:

- Like the shabby podium, carafe of water, and rambling, inaccurate introduction which assert that a particular person deserves to be listened to when giving a public lecture, footnotes confer authority on a writer.
- To the inexpert, footnotes look like deep root systems, solid and fixed; to the connoisseur, however, they reveal themselves as anthills, swarming with constructive and combative activity.
- Presumably the footnote's rise to high social, if not typographical, position took place when it became legitimate, after history and philology, its parents, finally married.

Pouring forth a bubbling stream of metaphors, analogies, and personifications, Grafton compares footnotes to podiums and water jugs (shabby markers of academic authority), to root systems and anthills (emblems of scholarly inertia and hyperactivity, respectively), and to an illegitimate child socially elevated by the parents' marriage. His own footnotes, however—ranging from terse source citations to lengthy tracts of German or Latin—are models of scholarly seriousness and decorum.

Unfortunately, many of the notes in academic books and articles today can be described neither as ironic commentaries nor as glittering rhetorical jewels:

> I refer not to the named or to the unnamed but still blatant (at least to the literate Hebrew reader) citations, evocations of works ranging from a seventh-century liturgy by Eleazar Ben Kallir (11; 15) to a twentieth-century Romantic masterpiece, H. N. Bialik's "The Pond" (תבךבת׳; 253; 229), but to some subtle echoes of the poetry of Israel's poet laureate, Natan Alterman (Hebrew ed., 16), unfortunately lost in translation. [Literary Studies endnote]
>
>   It seems natural if a common internalist posits a relation of instantiation (exemplification) and identifies it with U, or lets it play its ontological role (correspondingly, postulates relations of instantiation and identify them with, or lets them play the ontological roles of, U, U', U&", etc.). However, given that the problem of unity is not the problem of instantiation (cf. §2), this is an independent thesis and hence not an issue we need to consider. [Philosophy footnote]

As Grafton laments, pedantic notes such as these resemble "less the skilled work of a professional carrying out a precise function to a higher end than the offhand production and disposal of waste products."[11]

Researchers in disciplines outside the humanities do not suffer as badly as their arts-based cohorts from the spilled sewage of excessive marginalia. Nor do they tend to indulge in over-quotation, another tic of humanities scholars, whose respect for other writers' exact phraseology sometimes ties their own syntax up in knots:

> As Lisa Cody has argued in relation to the "spectacle" of the man-midwife, the urgent need for reproduction removed generation from the exclusive realm of feminine expertise and resituated it as a category "of 'universal' and 'public' interest to 'men and women.'" [Literary Studies]

The parenthetical citation systems favored by scientists and social scientists, however, provide no better guarantee of syntactical concision or stylistic hygiene than the note-based citation systems preferred in the arts. Madigan, Johnson, and Linton argue that, by encouraging authors to paraphrase rather than quote, APA style improves the "flow and feel of the resulting text."[12] Yet one could hardly argue that the following example "flows," except in the most disagreeable sense:

> In contrast to the research using questionnaires and experience sampling methods, studies using emotional stimuli have found that individuals with schizophrenia show normal reports of affective experience, such that individuals with schizophrenia and control participants report similar patterns of valence and arousal in their self-report ratings of their experience of emotional stimuli (e.g., Berenbaum & Oltmanns, 1992; Crespo-Facorro et al., 2001; Curtis, Lebow, Lake, Katsanis, & Iacono, 1999; Hempel et al., 2005; Kring, Kerr, Smith, & Neale, 1993; Kring & Neale, 1996; Matthews & Barch, 2004; Moberg et al., 2003; Quirk, Strauss, & Sloan, 1998; Rupp et al., 2005; Schlenker, Cohen, & Hopmann, 1995), although some studies showed differences between individuals with schizophrenia and control participants in terms of absolute levels of experience for both positive and negative stimuli (Crespo-Facorro et al., 2001; Curtis et al., 1999; Moberg et al., 2003; Plailly, d'Amato, Saoud, & Royet, 2006; Quirk et al., 1998).

The authors of this psychology article have taken an already bloated sentence (seventy-seven words) and stuffed no fewer than sixteen separate citations (seventy-three words) into its distended belly. The main problem here, as in much academic writing, is that they are simply trying to pack too much detail—some essential, some peripheral—into a single sentence, rather than making each point separately. As a first step toward improvement, the authors could strip away redundancies: the words *studies, control participants,* and *individuals with schizophrenia* all appear at least twice in the sentence, and *experience* occurs four times. Next, they could break the sentence up into two or three shorter ones, each with relevant citations at the end. Finally, they could read the revised passage aloud to each other—including the citations—and check for any phrases or interruptions that might trip up their readers.

Lengthy parenthetical citations violate, or at least risk violating, two key principles of stylish writing. First, they slow the text's momentum: how can you possibly tell a compelling research story if you have to stop and cough every few seconds? Second, much in the same way that discursive footnotes and endnotes lend themselves to eruptions of excessive erudition, parenthetical styles encourage extravagant but often meaningless name-dropping. Commentators ranging from legal scholar Steve Wise to historian David Henige to paleontologist Stephen K. Donovan have roundly criticized the scholarly practice—pervasive in the sciences and social sciences but virtually unheard of in the humanities—of citing articles, books, and even entire multivolume editions without designating specific page numbers.[13] This tendency, Henige notes, turns on its head the disciplinary stereotype that "scientists are sceptical souls" while humanists are "more trusting and forgiving, more tuned in to the fallibilities of their fellows":

> Particularly disconcerting is the disconnect between this unconcern with precision in citation and the extraordinary care taken to assure that submitted papers measure up in other ways. For, unlike these other factors—experimental rigour, quantitative accuracy, logical consistency, attention to lists of references—it appears that authors' citational scrupulousness is simply taken for granted.[14]

In my census of source citations and footnotes in articles from ten academic disciplines, I found that the anthropologists cited on average seventy-five sources per paper, whereas the computer scientists cited only twenty-seven, even though articles in both disciplines tend to have similar page lengths (see Figure 2.2 in Chapter 2). Similarly, in an analysis of citation conventions in eight academic disciplines, sociolinguist Ken Hyland found that sociologists include on average 104 source citations per paper, whereas physicists cite only about twenty-five times per paper.

Hyland notes that scientists typically introduce citations using "research verbs" *(showed, observed, developed)*, whereas philosophers favor "interpretive verbs" *(think, believe, overlook, fail)*. Tellingly, whom to cite turns out to be as important a consideration for many researchers as how to cite. As one of Hyland's interview subjects, a sociologist, explains:

> I've aligned myself with a particular camp and tend to cite people from there. Partly because I've been influenced by those ideas and partly because I want them to read my work. It's a kind of code, showing where I am on the spectrum. Where I stand.[15]

In a separate study, Hyland found that 70 percent of the papers he examined (240 articles from eight different disciplines) contained at least one reference to the author's own work. Scientists and engineers, in particular, self-cite frequently, both to establish their disciplinary credibility and to build up a coherent research profile.[16] As Hyland's research confirms, citational practices are closely entwined with disciplinary protocols and identities. At their worst, they offer a potential platform for academic hubris, encouraging rampant name-dropping, self-promotion, and other forms of intellectual self-indulgence. At their best, however, citation conventions promote academic humility and generosity; they remind researchers to guard against plagiarism, to acknowledge their intellectual debts, and to affirm the contributions of their peers.

THINGS TO TRY

- If you have a choice of citation styles, carefully weigh your options. List the pros and cons of each style you are considering (for example, MLA versus Chicago or APA versus Harvard) and make an informed decision based on *your* priorities and preferences.
- If you have no choice of citation styles, take control of the situation by establishing your own key principles for employing the required style. For example:

- If the style allows footnotes or endnotes, do you want your
  notes to be long and discursive or brief and informative?
  Can you justify your choice? (The fact that other scholars
  in your field favor one option or the other is not, on its
  own, a sufficiently compelling reason.)
- If you are using an in-text citation style such as MLA, do
  you need footnotes at all? (Just because they are conventional in your field does not necessarily mean they are
  required; many editors in fact discourage discursive notes.)
- Will your list of sources function as a full bibliography,
  naming every book or article ever published on your
  research topic, or as a "Works Cited" section, listing only
  those works that you actually mention in the main text?
  (Your response will no doubt be influenced by disciplinary
  conventions, but need not be ruled by them.)

- Whenever possible, compose your book or article from the
  outset in the citation style you plan to use for final publication. For peer-reviewed articles, use the house style of
  the journal to which you intend to submit the article first.
- Read all of your discursive notes and/or parenthetical
  citations aloud. Can you trim them, polish them, move
  them into the main text, or position them less obtrusively?

CHAPTER 13

THE BIG PICTURE

If you ask a roomful of academics to characterize stylish academic writing, at least a few will inevitably reply that the authors they most admire are those who "express complex ideas clearly." Some might embellish the point, noting that stylish academic writers express complex ideas clearly and *succinctly*, clearly and *elegantly*, clearly and *engagingly*, or clearly and *persuasively*. Others will propose variations, stating that stylish academic writers express complex ideas in language that *aids* the reader's understanding or *challenges* the reader's understanding or *extends* the reader's understanding. Central to all these definitions, despite their differing nuances, is the elusive art of abstraction; that is, the stylish academic writer's ability to paint a big picture on a small canvas, sketching the contours of an intricate argument in just a few broad strokes.

Paradoxically, the most effective academic *abstracts*—a noun I use in this chapter to designate any summary statement of academic purpose, such as a grant proposal, article synopsis, or book prospectus—are often highly *concrete*, harnessing the language of the senses as well as the language of the mind. Performance scholar Sally Banes, for example, uses the sensual word "stink" to communicate the physical and symbolic importance of odor in Western theater:

For a century at least, in Western cultures, strong odors were mostly regarded as "bad," stinks to be done away with. Banes finds that performing artists are attempting to restore the sense of smell to the theatrical experience. She anatomizes the rhetoric and practice of "aroma design" in theatrical representation and looks at smell as a paradigm of "liveness."[1]

Similarly, psychologists Thomas Carnahan and Sam McFarland invoke real people and places (students, guards, Abu Ghraib) in their study of the psychological dispositions that underlie abusive behavior:

> The authors investigated whether students who selectively volunteer for a study of prison life possess dispositions associated with behaving abusively. Students were recruited for a psychological study of prison life using a virtually identical newspaper ad as used in the Stanford Prison Experiment (SPE; Haney, Banks & Zimbardo, 1973) or for a psychological study, an identical ad minus the words of prison life. Volunteers for the prison study scored significantly higher on measures of the abuse-related dispositions of aggressiveness, authoritarianism, Machiavellianism, narcissism, and social dominance and lower on empathy and altruism, two qualities inversely related to aggressive abuse. . . . Implications for interpreting the abusiveness of American military guards at Abu Ghraib Prison also are discussed.[2]

These two otherwise very different abstracts are clear, direct, and to the point, albeit rather impersonal ("Banes finds," "the authors investigated") and passively phrased ("strong odors were mostly regarded," "implications . . . are discussed"). Nouns and verbs sit close together so we know exactly who is doing what: *"performing artists are attempting," "the authors investigated," "volunteers* for the prison study *scored."* Both abstracts contain vocabulary that might challenge a nonacademic reader *(anatomizes, paradigm, Machiavellianism, narcissism)*. However, the authors steer clear of the kind of arcane, opaque, discipline-specific jargon that demands highly specialized subject knowledge.

MALCOLM COULTHARD

For forty years linguists have talked about idiolect and the uniqueness of individual utterances. This article explores how far these two concepts can be used to answer certain questions about the authorship of written documents—for instance how similar can two student essays be before one begins to suspect plagiarism? The article examines two ways of measuring similarity: the proportion of shared vocabulary and the number and length of shared phrases, and illustrates with examples drawn from both actual criminal court cases and incidents of student plagiarism. The article ends by engaging with Solan and Tiersma's contribution to this volume and considering whether such forensic linguistic evidence would be acceptable in American courts as well as how it might successfully be presented to a lay audience.

In his abstract for an article titled "Author Identification, Idiolect, and Linguistic Uniqueness," linguist Malcolm Coulthard eschews the complex syntax and specialized vocabulary beloved by so many other researchers in his field. Aside from some sloppy punctuation, his sentences are clear and well structured, laying out the various questions that his article attempts to answer and foreshadowing his use of concrete examples from both the college classroom and the criminal court. Coulthard's article opens with an anecdote about a man accused of murder based on incriminating statements that forensic analysts later proved to have been forged by police. Fittingly, Coulthard structures his own work something like a mystery story or courtroom drama; rather than delivering his thesis up front, he waits until the final paragraph to deliver his verdict. Yes, he eventually concludes, the concepts of *idiolect* and *linguistic uniqueness* (phrases that he carefully defines at the beginning of the article) are indeed robust, providing a basis for answering "with a high degree of confidence" important forensic questions about authorship.

Compare the above examples with the following abstract, which appeared in a leading higher education research journal:

Policy in higher education suggests that curriculum should be more responsive to economist arguments than was the case in the past. Although some guidance has been given to how to develop more work-integrated curricula, little attention has been given to interactions in meetings between workplace and academic representatives in which issues of curriculum development are discussed. As such there appears to be a gap in current curriculum theory. The author suggests that such interactions may be fruitfully examined using concepts derived from studies in the sociology of science and organizational dynamics. Such analyses may contribute to understanding what conditions enable productive interactions, which may be the development of hybrid objects and languages which speak to both groupings. .

The article addresses a topic that could presumably be of interest to academics from many different disciplines: how can faculty, especially those in professionally oriented fields, engage in more productive conversations about course and curriculum design with the people who will eventually hire their students? The author, however, makes no attempt to invite such readers to the table. The abstract is dry, impersonal, wordy, and vague, filled with agency-free claims ("some guidance has been given"—by whom?), hedging maneuvers ("*appears* to be," "*may* be," "*may* contribute"), and syntactically fuzzy sentences ("Such analyses may contribute to understanding what conditions enable productive interactions, which may be the development of hybrid objects and languages which speak to both groupings"—the first *which* has no clear referent, and the second *which* should be *that*). Aside from "the author," no human beings appear anywhere in the abstract, unless we count the shadowy "workplace and academic representatives" whose interactions "*may* be fruitfully examined"—but *will* they be examined here, or will the article merely circle around them, as the abstract does? Rather than rendering complex ideas clear and comprehensible, the author has taken a rather simple idea—sociological concepts can teach us how to run better meetings—and twisted it into a discursive pretzel.

The purpose of a scholarly abstract is not merely to *summarize* an article's content but to *persuade* one's discipline-based peers that the research is important and the article is therefore worth reading.[3] In the higher education abstract quoted above, the author makes plenty of insider moves, including the obligatory claim that his article, like a thumb artfully inserted into a leaky dike, will plug a "gap" in the existing scholarship. Yet the abstract lacks persuasive power—not in spite of, but precisely because of, its adherence to disciplinary conventions. The art of persuasion necessarily involves human conversation; indeed, the *Oxford English Dictionary* defines persuasion as "the addressing of arguments or appeals *to a person* [my emphasis] in order to induce cooperation, submission, or agreement."[4] Authors who adopt an impersonal, "academic" tone are neglecting one of the most powerfully persuasive tools at the stylish writer's disposal: the human touch.

In the social sciences and humanities, researchers can draw readers into their argument by giving a voice and presence to human subjects: for example, the performance artists discussed by Banes or the students involved in Carnahan and McFarland's psychology experiments. Scientists who study nonhuman subjects can make their research accessible in other ways, such as by using first-person pronouns ("*we* approached") to signal the researchers' presence in the work:

All birds dropping hard-bodied prey face a trade-off. It is likely that the impact damage to the prey increases as drop height increases, as this will influence the speed at which the prey hits the ground, and so the energy it experiences on impact. However, the time and energy costs of flight also increase with increasing drop heights. Furthermore, if a bird drops a prey item more than once, it incurs additional time and energy costs while landing, retrieving the prey item and taking off again. The main aim of this paper, therefore, is to examine how this trade-off influences decisions taken by birds dropping hard-bodied prey. We approached this problem in two ways.[5]

Note the many ways in which the authors of this article—titled "The Economics of Getting High: Decisions Made by Common Gulls Dropping their Cockles to Open Them"—engage and inform their readers. They begin by clearly defining the problem that motivates their research: "All birds dropping hard-bodied prey face a trade-off." In verb-driven sentences filled with concrete nouns, they vividly describe the gulls in flight and the hard-bodied objects they drop from on high. If we are persuaded to read beyond the abstract, it is because the authors have conveyed not only the arc of their research but its essence. Rather than taking elementary concepts and spinning them out in complex language, they have achieved the stylish writer's nirvana: "complex ideas clearly expressed."

The following grid, adapted from one developed by higher education researcher David Green, offers one way to visualize the various registers into which academic writing typically falls:[6]

	Simple Ideas	Complex Ideas
Clear Language		
Difficult Language		

While some academics may stray between two or more sections of the grid—for example, writing a simple and clear abstract followed by a complex and difficult opening paragraph—the stylish academic writers quoted throughout this book mostly gravitate toward the top right-hand corner: complex ideas communicated in clear, comprehensible language. There is, of course, a

STEPHEN K. DONOVAN

The libraries of universities and other research institutions are home to an abundance of academic journals, published in multifarious sizes, thicknesses, languages, and formats, with covers varying from black to psychedelic and covering every subject imaginable. More uniformity of format would favour the author, who would no longer have to tailor style to wherever the latest contribution is being submitted, but the current diversity of formats is aimed at the reader. Long may it so remain.

Paleontologist Stephen K. Donovan—whose publications include books with titles like *Jamaican Rock Stars, 1823–1971: The Geologists Who Explored Jamaica*—brings both a scientist's clarity and a stylish writer's panache to this compact yet engaging three-sentence abstract, the teaser for an article in the *Journal of Scholarly Publishing*.

In the first sentence, Donovan teleports us into the physical space of the university library and invites us to picture what we will find there: academic journals of various sizes and thicknesses, with covers ranging from "black to psychedelic." Despite its concrete imagery, however, this opening line also conveys an abstract argument: the diversity of the journal covers, Donovan implies, mirrors the diversity of their intellectual coverage.

In the second sentence, Donovan sets up the conflict that his article will explore at length: uniformity of format favors the author, he argues, while diversity of format favors the reader. He ends by forthrightly declaring his own allegiance to the diversity camp. A less-confident author might have spun out a laborious, jargon-studded thesis sentence: "This article analyzes the conflicting claims of both the writerly and readerly paradigms, concluding that the readerly benefits of material and epistemological variety should be given precedence over the writerly convenience afforded by stylistic standardization." Instead, Donovan ends by summing up in just five words his argument that diversity should be defended: "Long may it so remain."

place in the world for simple ideas expressed in simple language—
for example, in a primary school textbook or a government-
issued voting manual—and academics in fields such as literary
studies or philosophy may argue for the educational and intellectual value of complex ideas expressed in rich, challenging
language. But can anyone justify expressing simple ideas in difficult language? Green's grid offers a useful starting point not
only for evaluating other academics' writing, but for honestly
assessing one's own.

Condensing a complex research project into a pithy abstract
is no simple task, to be sure. An even greater challenge is to boil
that abstract down into an "elevator statement": the seemingly
off-the-cuff but in fact brilliantly polished single-sentence summary that you offer to the colleague who turns to you in the elevator at an academic conference and asks, "So what are you working on?" You have just a minute or two to respond: the time that
it takes for the elevator to arrive at its destination floor. Stylish
academic writers often offer an elevator statement of sorts at the
start of their scholarly books or articles, as a means of engaging
their readers' attention and inspiring them to continue reading:

> This is a book about plots and plotting, about how stories come to
> be ordered in significant form, and also about our desire and need
> for such orderings.[7]
>
> This book is about the impact of trauma both on individuals and
> on entire cultures or nations and about the need to share and "trans-
> late" such traumatic impact.[8]
>
> As I shall try to show in this book, human language has a com-
> plexity and creativity that is unmatched by any other form of animal
> communication, and probably depends on completely different
> principles.[9]

Note that each of these opening statements describes not only
the book's subject but its argument, not only its *what* but its
why. Literary scholar Peter Brooks promises to explain *why* we

JONATHAN CULLER

I began work on this topic for a conference at the University of London on style in philosophy. The organizers suggested that I address the question of what it is for a piece of philosophy to be badly written—no doubt thinking that as a reader of French philosophers, I would have special expertise on this question or at least a lot of relevant experience. In fact, I was happy to take up this question because I have been intrigued of late by claims made in the world of Anglophone philosophy about bad writing. The journal *Philosophy and Literature* . . . had for several years announced a Bad Writing Award, and since this award had recently been conferred on a sentence by Judith Butler that appeared in *Diacritics* during my stint as editor, I had a personal interest in the concept of bad writing in philosophy and the criteria of selection.

Literary scholar Jonathan Culler is a study in paradox: an apologist for "difficult" writing who himself is a master of determinedly lucid prose. Here, in the opening paragraph of an essay titled "Bad Writing and Good Philosophy," he engages his readers' attention and sympathy by establishing both his personal interest and his professional stake in the topic of "bad writing." Next, he provides an extended gloss of cultural theorist Judith Butler's prizewinning ninety-three-word sentence, which contains twenty-eight abstract nouns but no concrete language whatsoever, aside from invocations of "structure" and "structural totalities." Culler generously concludes that Butler's sentence is in fact "quite pedagogic writing. Key points are rephrased and repeated so that if you don't catch on the first time around, you have another chance when they come by again." In Culler's evocative phrasing, Butler's disorienting syntax becomes a spinning merry-go-round with a gold ring held out to the persistent reader.

tell stories; cultural theorist E. Ann Kaplan investigates *why* we feel compelled to share and transform traumatic events through literature and art; and psycholinguist Michael Corballis explores *why* human language has evolved to be so complex and creative.

The secret ingredient of an effective elevator statement—or, for that matter, of a persuasive abstract, article, or book—is a strong *thesis* or *argument*. Both words are frequently heard in the freshman composition classroom but seldom in the research laboratory. However, identical principles apply in both venues: writers who put forth a bold, defensible claim are much more likely to generate engaging, persuasive prose than those who offer bland statements of fact with which no one could possibly disagree. In the sciences and social sciences, a strong thesis follows naturally from a compelling *research question,* as when a group of behavioralists ask how seagulls solve the height versus energy problem when dropping cockles onto the rocks below. Some academics may resist the notion that a complex argument can always be reduced to a single sentence; with poet and literary critic Charles Bernstein, they might even decry the "epistemological positivism" of an academic environment in which "one's work is supposed to be easily summed up, definable, packaged, polished, wrinkles and contradictions eliminated, digressions booted" and in which "dissertations must not violate stylistic norms because that might jeopardize our young scholar's future."[10] Yet it is worth noting that even Bernstein's polemic against academic conformism (which contains plenty of wrinkles, contradictions, and digressions of its own) can be summed up, elevator-style, in a persuasive thesis statement: Prevailing stylistic conventions, Bernstein argues, inhibit scholarly inquiry and stifle innovation.

For stylish academic writers, clarity and complexity are bedfellows, not rivals. Evolutionary biologist Richard Dawkins, who for more than a decade held the post of Professor for Public

Understanding of Science at Oxford University, offers the following advice to scientists:

> Do not talk down. Try to inspire everybody with the poetry of science and make your explanations as easy as honesty allows, but at the same time do not neglect the difficult. Put extra effort into explaining to those readers prepared to put matching effort into understanding.[11]

Dawkins's formula can be adapted by academics in any field. Researchers who master the art of abstraction—the ability to express complex ideas clearly—will enlighten and persuade not only nonspecialist audiences but their discipline-based colleagues well.

THINGS TO TRY

- Use David Green's grid to rate examples of academic writing that you particularly admire or dislike. (For "clear" and "difficult," you can substitute "easy to read" and "hard to read," "lucid" and "opaque," "illuminating" and "bewildering," or any other oppositional adjectives that you find helpful). Most likely you will find that the best writers in your field inhabit the "complex but clear" box, whereas those whose work you find hard to digest employ convoluted language either to express complex concepts or, more problematically, to obfuscate simple ideas. Be honest with yourself: Which grid does your own work fall into?
- Answer the following questions in simple, conversational language, avoiding disciplinary jargon:
  - What is the *main point* of your article, dissertation, or book? (Why is it important, whether to you or to anyone else?)
  - Who is your intended *audience?*
  - What *research question(s)* do you aim to answer?

- What new *contribution(s)* does your research make to theory? to practice?
- What is your overarching *thesis* or *argument?*
- What *evidence* do you offer in support?

Keep your responses close at hand as you construct your summary statement, which should answer most if not all of these questions, especially the first one ("What's the point?").

- Make sure your abstract contains the following:

  - Clear, well-structured sentences in which nouns and their modifying verbs sit close together.
  - At least a few concrete nouns and/or verbs.
  - A touch of humanity: for example, first-person pronouns *(I/we),* real people (research subjects, other researchers), or language that grounds abstract ideas in human experience.
  - A contestable thesis or argument.

- Show your abstract to a few trusted friends or colleagues, both from within and outside your discipline. Ask them to give you candid answers to the following questions:

  - Do you understand what my research is about and why it's important?
  - Does my abstract make you want to keep reading?

CHAPTER 14

THE CREATIVE TOUCH

Take a gamine teenager, dress her in a sheath frock and elbow-length gloves, thrust a cigarette holder into her hand, and still she will not look like Audrey Hepburn. Some elements of stylishness defy definition or imitation, no matter how hard we try. As novelist Willa Cather puts it:

> The qualities of a first-rate writer cannot be defined, but only experienced. It is just the thing in him which escapes analysis that makes him first-rate. One can catalogue all the qualities that he shares with other writers, but the thing that is his very own, his timbre, this cannot be defined any more than the quality of a beautiful speaking voice can be.[1]

Nonetheless, this chapter investigates that elusive *je ne sais quoi* of stylish writing: the cluster of special qualities that make certain writers stand out from the crowd. These include passion, commitment, pleasure, playfulness, humor, elegance, lyricism, originality, imagination, creativity, and "undisciplined thinking"—attributes that are easy enough to recognize (perhaps because they occur so rarely in academic writing) but difficult to define or emulate.

Passion and commitment are stylistic qualities that academic writers often praise in other people's writing but suppress in their own. Most academics would describe themselves as passionate, committed researchers; they love what they do and undertake

CHRISTOPHER GREY AND AMANDA SINCLAIR

The speaker begins. His topic is "managerial regimes of truth," a subject I am very interested in. We are five minutes in and I'm beginning to feel dizzy. . . . Foucault and Derrida have been dismissed as old hat, Zizek as a suspect popularist, Deleuze—no I haven't been paying attention, I am not sure whether he is in favour or out. Hardt and Negri show promise but have essentialist "tendencies." It's rather like a show trial in those more literal regimes of truth, where the accused have been drugged and the witnesses given a script to follow. . . . The words are coming more quickly now, as the Chair has indicated that time is short and I notice that the speaker is only on his first slide and has—can it be eight?—eight more to get through. What is the point of this, I wonder, what are you really trying to say? And then I realize what the speaker is saying. He is saying that he has read a great deal more than anyone else.

In a withering, often hilarious critique of the "pompous, impenetrable" prose that dominates their discipline, Christopher Grey (professor of organizational theory at Cambridge University) and Amanda Sinclair (professor of management at Melbourne Business School) call for their colleagues in critical management studies to imagine writing differently. What's more, they demonstrate how it can be done. Through an artful blend of satire, polemic, personal reflection, and fantasy, their article "Writing Differently" expresses their aesthetic, moral, and political concerns about "pretentious, obscurantist" writing. Both authors acknowledge the risks involved in writing differently, especially for academics "in more marginalized positions or at the start of their careers." But they insist on the importance of trying:

We want writing to be taken seriously, as powerful and evocative performance, able to change people's experiences of the world, rather than as a shriven, cowed and cowering path towards routinized, professionalized "publication."

their work with a strong sense of personal engagement. Many actively desire to make a difference in the world, whether by finding a cure for a deadly disease, by enlarging our understanding of natural and cultural phenomena, or by changing the way people think. Yet these same researchers have typically been trained, either implicitly or explicitly, to strip all emotion from their academic writing. What would happen if they allowed even a modicum of the passion they feel to color their prose?

Openly impassioned writing is most frequently found in disciplines that favor a personal voice and a partisan viewpoint: for example, in fields where queer, feminist, and postcolonial perspectives (among others) have encouraged academics to integrate identity politics into their scholarship. In an article on indigenous epistemologies in the Pacific Islands, anthropologist David Gegeo candidly confesses to have been "taken somewhat off-guard" by the comments of a reviewer who perceived Gegeo's anticolonialist scholarship as intellectually passé:

> The individualistic, careerist approach of Anglo-European scholarship means that after publishing a few articles or maybe a book on the topic, the scholar moves on to something else. . . . The perspective of a growing number of us Pacific Islands scholars, however, is to approach research from a *communitarian perspective*: that is, research that is not only applied (targeted to making positive changes) but is firmly anchored in Indigenous or Native epistemologies and methodologies.[2]

In a similar vein, Bronwyn Davies, a feminist educational scholar, offers a personal anecdote to frame her critical analysis of neoliberal discourse in contemporary academic institutions:

> At the beginning of my academic life my Head of Department prevaricated about promoting me from tutor to temporary lecturer. After weeks of waiting I asked him had he made up his mind, and he told me it was a difficult decision to make, since in his view women should remain in service positions. . . . My point here is not to sneer at his old fashioned narrow mindedness, but to comprehend how it

is that discourses colonize us—gifting us with our existence and shaping our desires, our beliefs in what is right—the things we are prepared to die for.[3]

These scholars are frankly passionate about their work, but not in a sloppily emotive way. Quite the opposite; the intensity of their emotions motivates them to theorize, criticize, and methodically subvert the epistemological paradigms within which their research operates.

Passionate prose is, however, by no means exclusively the purview of politically engaged humanists and social sciences who write in the first person. Academics in any field can express passion for their subject matter, drawing on a range of rhetorical techniques that need not necessarily include a personal voice. In a heartfelt plea for their colleagues in the health sector to resist "magical thinking" about the benefits of computerization, information technologists Carol Diamond and Clay Shirky build up emotional intensity through repetition ("Success is"), alliteration ("days instead of decades"), and metaphors *(tool, goal):*

> IT [information technology] is a tool, not a goal. Success should not be measured by the number of hospitals with computerized order entry systems or patients with electronic personal health records. Success is when clinical outcomes improve. Success is when everyone can learn which methods and treatments work, and which don't, in days instead of decades.[4]

Similarly, in a 2002 article written entirely in the third person and filled with typically academic hedging words *(may, seem),* cognitive biologist Ladislav Kováč injects a strong sense of personal engagement into his analysis of the scientific aftermath of the terrorist attacks of September 11, 2001:

> Does the terrorism of the twenty-first century have common roots with the totalitarism of the twentieth century? Is not one of the reasons of its upsurge the fact that humankind has not achieved a proper understanding of the very nature of Nazism and Communism and has not drawn consequential conclusions? Should not science,

the paragon of rationality, take up this state of the world affairs as a warning and as a challenge?[5]

Through a series of rhetorical questions that gradually increase in interrogative force (from *does* and *is* to *should*), Kováč conveys his passionate conviction that the science community has not responded appropriately to the threat of global terrorism.

Passion's partner is *pleasure:* the sense of pure enjoyment that a researcher feels upon making a new discovery; that a writer feels upon producing a well-turned phrase; and that a reader feels upon encountering an innovative idea, a perfect sentence, or, ideally, the former couched within the latter. As Roland Barthes observes in *The Pleasure of the Text,* "If I read this sentence, this story, or this word with pleasure, it is because they were written in pleasure."[6] Some stylish academics—Barthes himself is a prime example—communicate such an intense, almost giddy pleasure in and through their writing that only the most curmudgeonly of readers could fail to be carried along by it. Cognitive scientist Douglas Hofstadter, in his book *Gödel, Escher, Bach,* expresses his "enthusiasm and reverence for certain ideas" in language suffused with intellectual delight, even awe:

> One of the most remarkable and difficult-to-describe qualities of consciousness is visual imagery. How do we create a visual image out of our living room? Of a roaring mountain brook? Of an orange? Even more mysterious, how do we manufacture images unconsciously, images which guide our thoughts, giving them power and color and depth? From what store are they fetched? What magic allows us to mesh two or three images, hardly giving a thought as to how we should do it?[7]

Likewise, mathematician Martin Gardner opens his book *The Ambidextrous Universe* by inviting readers to see the world through the eyes of an innocent:

> There is no better way to begin this book than by trying to see your image in the mirror with something like the wonder and curiosity of a chimpanzee.[8]

DOUGLAS HOFSTADTER

Only at [the typesetting] stage did the book's unusual stylistic hallmarks really emerge—the sometimes-silly playing with words, the concocting of novel verbal structures that imitate musical forms, the wallowing in analogies of every sort, the spinning of stories whose very structures exemplify the points they are talking about, the mixing of oddball personalities in fantastic scenarios. As I was writing, I certainly knew that my book would be quite different from other books on related topics, and that I was violating quite a number of conventions. Nonetheless I blithely continued, because I felt confident that what I was doing simply had to be done, and that it had an intrinsic rightness to it.

In 1973, as a twenty-eight-year-old PhD student in physics, Douglas Hofstadter started writing the manuscript that would eventually become *Gödel, Escher, Bach: An Eternal Golden Braid*. Published in 1979, Hofstadter's 777-page treatise on "fugues and canons, logic and truth, geometry, recursion, syntactic structures, the nature of meaning, Zen Buddhism, paradoxes, brain and mind, reductionism and holism, ant colonies, concepts and mental representations, translation, computers and their languages, DNA, proteins, the genetic code, artificial intelligence, creativity, consciousness and free will [and] sometimes even art and music" won the 1980 Pulitzer Prize for general nonfiction and has since been translated into numerous languages. Hofstadter typeset the entire volume himself, cramming it full of examples, anecdotes, visual images, theorems, proofs, jokes, puns, and "strange loops" of various kinds. From its highly inventive chapter and section titles ("BlooP and FlooP and GlooP," "Birthday Cantatatata") and its unusual structure (a counterpoint between Dialogues and Chapters), right down to its wry acknowledgments ("Thanks to Marsha Meredith for being the meta-author of a droll kōan"), the entire book—like Hofstadter's subsequent research on artificial intelligence, translation, recursive language, and other topics—is an exercise in creative thinking and academic nonconformity.

Not everyone will be charmed by such flights of enthusiasm; some academics might even feel condescended to by a writer who asks them to think like a monkey. All the same, for most readers, there is something appealingly engaging about an academic writer who unabashedly seeks to give and receive pleasure through language and ideas.

That pleasure might or might not manifest itself through humor—amusing anecdotes, clever puns—and other forms of verbal playfulness (dare I say *fun?*). Stylish writers who spice up their work with humor generally do so with a light touch; any good teacher knows how efficiently humor can energize a classroom but also how easily a half-cocked joke can misfire. At its best, humor engages our bodies in the robustly physical ceremony of laughter. At its worst, a poorly executed witticism exposes the author's own folly. The safest forms of academic humor (examples of which can be found in many of the "Spotlight on Style" callouts scattered throughout this book) are also the most subtle: the wry aside, the satirical riff, the unexpected turn of phrase.

And then there is *elegance,* a stylistic attribute that can coexist with passion and humor or flourish on its own. In the world of fashion and design, elegance suggests a "refined grace of form and movement, tastefulness of adornment, refined luxury." In science, elegance aligns with precision, concision, and "ingenious simplicity": an elegant solution is the one that maps the most efficient route through complex terrain. Humanities scholars often use the word "elegant" as an ill-defined synonym for "well written." More helpfully, the *Oxford English Dictionary* defines literary elegance as "tasteful correctness, harmonious simplicity, in the choice and arrangement of words."[9] An elegant writer, then, is one who makes us feel that every word has been perfectly chosen, as when James D. Watson and Francis Crick first described the double-helical structure of DNA:

> We wish to put forward a radically different structure for the salt of dioxyribose nucleic acid. This structure has two helical chains each

coiled round the same axis (see diagram). . . . The two chains (but not their bases) are related by a dyad perpendicular to the fibre axis. Both chains follow right-handed helixes, but owing to the dyad the sequences of the atoms in the two chains run in opposite directions.

Toward the end of their famously economical 985-word paper in the journal *Nature,* Watson and Crick drily note: "It has not escaped our notice that the specific pairing we have postulated immediately suggests a possible copying mechanism for the genetic material."[10] Rather than crowing about having cracked the code of life, they opt for the rhetorical trope of *litotes,* or elegant understatement.

In some cases, elegance manifests itself through clarity and concision; in others, it is achieved through lyricism, an author's use of unabashedly expressive language to build up the kind of emotional intensity and semantic density more commonly associated with poetry than with academic prose. Lyricism flowers most freely in the work of academics who are themselves poets, such as literary scholar Selina Tusitala Marsh or educational researcher Cynthia Dillard, both of whom strategically incorporate their own poetry into their scholarly writing: "Beginning with my own voice has become a political act," declares Marsh, "as I straddle the border between theory and creativity."[11] However, poetic interludes can be found in the research publications of nearly every academic discipline, as when biologist Julian Vincent, in an otherwise highly technical article on phenolic tanning, waxes eloquent about the fossilized forewings of beetles— "Bits of beetle elytron can be found, pristine, in drift deposits of a million or more years old"—or when historian of science John Heilbron layers a thick slathering of purple prose onto his otherwise restrained description of solar observatories in medieval churches:[12]

> The lighting up of a special place by a flash from heaven at a preset time can make an impression even on ordinary minds. The tourists who happen to be in San Petronio when the sun plays like a searchlight

across the rosy pavement tarry for longer than the five minutes they had allotted to the cathedral to watch a display of whose purpose and author they have not an inkling.[13]

Heilbron's uncharacteristically extravagant language—the heaven-sent flash of light, the sun playing like a searchlight, the rosy pavement, the tarrying tourists—communicates not only his own passion for his subject but also his desire to instill a similar sense of joy and wonder in his readers. Every word has been carefully chosen, like the words of a poem, for its weight, sound, and resonance.

Stylish authors such as Vincent and Heilbron borrow many verbal techniques—assonance, alliteration, onomatopoeia—from the literary mode we label "creative writing." And why shouldn't they? Few academics would disagree that innovative research requires creativity, originality, and imagination as well as hard work and skill: "one per cent inspiration, ninety-nine per cent perspiration," to borrow Thomas Edison's famous description of genius.[14] Yet academics in most disciplines have been trained to be critical rather than creative thinkers, with little opportunity for merging the two modes. Fortunately, numerous resources and strategies are available—some playful and unconventional, others rational and self-reflexive—for writers who want to shift outside their comfort zone and develop the creative side of their intellect.[15]

"Be creative!" is not, to be sure, an easy command to obey at will. It is made even more challenging when the words "Be disciplined!" are expelled in the very same breath. Interdisciplinarity—or what we might call "undisciplined thinking"—turns out to be the surprise ingredient in the stylish writer's repertoire: a trait I was not looking for when I started researching this book but have noticed over again in the work of academic authors whose writing is praised by their peers. Evolutionary biologist Richard Dawkins opens his book *Climbing Mount Impossible* with an account of a literary lecture on figs; psychologist Robert

DANIEL DENNETT

Cognitive scientists themselves are often just as much in the grip of the sorts of misapprehensions and confusions as outsiders succumb to. . . . All of these experiments rely on subjects making a most unnatural judgment of simultaneity the import of which is not carefully analyzed, because of the presumption that the right question to ask is, *When does the subject become aware of the intention to act?* . . . This creates the illusion of an ominous temporal bottleneck, with the Conscious Agent impatiently waiting (in the Cartesian Theater) for news from the rest of the brain about what projects are underway. I must add that the literature on the topic by philosophers includes some that is equally ill considered. However, since better work is on the way, there is no need to dwell on past confusions.

In an interdisciplinary article titled "The Part of Cognitive Science That Is Philosophy," philosopher Daniel Dennett dives headfirst into the conceptual chasm that divides the sciences and the humanities. Arguing that "there is much good work for philosophers to do in cognitive science if they adopt the constructive attitude that prevails in science," he strokes the egos of his audience (mainly cognitive scientists) before going on to critique their "misapprehensions and confusions" about the relationship between conscious intentionality and action. Like many philosophers, Dennett writes in a first-person, informal voice, using rhetorical questions, conversational asides, and concrete imagery ("temporal bottleneck," "Cartesian Theater") to keep his readers on track. Sometimes, to be sure, his mixed metaphors get out of hand:

I once dismissed any theory that "replaced the little man in the brain with a committee" as conceptually bankrupt—until I realized that this was indeed a path, perhaps the royal road, to getting rid of the little man altogether. So live by the sword, die by the sword.

But perhaps it is better to die by the sword, a little man bankrupt on the royal road to excess, than to fade away from stylistic boredom.

Sternberg opens *Cupid's Arrow: The Course of Love through Time* with a Greek myth; cultural theorist Marjorie Garber opens *Academic Instincts* with an anecdote about the election of Jesse "The Body" Ventura as governor of Minnesota; psycholinguist Michael Corballis opens *Hand to Mouth: The Origins of Language* with a Dennis Glover poem about magpies; anthropologist Ruth Behar opens *The Vulnerable Observer: Anthropology That Breaks Your Heart* with a meditation on a short story by Isabel Allende.[16] These stylish academics read widely across disciplinary lines, and it shows. Equally important, they also *think* across disciplinary lines, as evidenced in the wide-ranging nature of their work. Chicken and egg are difficult to distinguish here: do these authors read widely because they are inherently interested in a variety of disciplines, or do they think across disciplines because they read so widely? Either way, their stylistic and conceptual elasticity is evident everywhere in their scholarly prose.

Stylish academics do not write "outside the box" merely for the sake of showing off their intellectual audacity and skill. Their aim is to communicate ideas and arguments to readers in the most effective and engaging way possible—even when doing so means defying disciplinary norms. Numerous studies have documented the crucial role of lateral thinking in the creative process: that is, the ability of pathbreaking researchers to "think sideways" rather than always plodding forward in a straight conceptual trajectory.[17] Academics who rigidly adhere to disciplinary conventions, never glancing to the right or left, risk repeating the fate of Dr. Seuss's North-Going Zax and South-Going Zax, who refused to move either a step to the east or a step to the west when they met, so that the two of them ended up stubbornly facing each other for years, unbudging, while cities and motorways sprang up around them and the rest of history moved forward.[18]

THINGS TO TRY

- "Read like a butterfly, write like a bee."[19] Novelist Philip Pullman exhorts writers to read widely and voraciously, without necessarily worrying about whether a given book or article will be useful to their current research. Later, you can make a conscious effort to integrate ideas drawn from your outside reading into your academic writing.

- *Freewriting* is a generative technique advocated by Peter Elbow and others as a quick and easy way to get your creative juices flowing:[20]

  - Grab a pen and paper (I favor high-quality fountain pens and attractively bound notebooks, but many writers are not so fussy), settle yourself someplace where you will not be disturbed (a park bench or café would be ideal, but an office with the door closed works just fine too), and resolve to write without interruption for a predetermined amount of time.

  - As you write, don't allow your pen to leave the paper for more than a few seconds at a time. Your goal is to keep writing continuously until your time is up, without stopping to correct errors, read over what you have just written, or polish your prose.

  - You may feel emotional barriers rising or falling and unexpected thoughts surging through your head. Whatever happens, keep writing. Afterward, you can shape your words into something more coherent—or not. The process, not the product, is the point of the exercise.

  Free drawing, mind mapping, and *verbal brainstorming* (for example, talking into a voice recorder) offer visual and oral alternatives to freewriting.

- Other suggestions for generating new ideas and perspectives.

  - Make a list of all the ways your research arouses your passion, stokes your commitments, and gives you pleasure.

- Write about the funny side, the absurd side, or even the dark side of your research project.
- Write a poem about your research—anything from a confessional poem about your own scholarly struggles to a series of haiku about your research subject.
- Choose a text, picture, or news item from outside your discipline—for example, a literary quotation, historical vignette, cartoon, scientific phenomenon, or movie plot—and freewrite for ten minutes about how you could incorporate that item into a presentation or publication about your research. What connections, however tenuous, can you draw?
- Ask a friend, relative, or small child to write down the name of a randomly chosen object—something specific enough that you can actually picture it: a fat dachshund, a red tulip. Freewrite for ten minutes about all the ways that object resembles your research project.
- Draw a picture of your research.
- Make a mind map of your research, starting with your central thesis or research question and working outward from there. (For more detailed instructions on mind mapping, see Tony Buzan's *Mind Map Book* or any of the many computer programs that include mind-mapping software).[21]
- Color code your research: for example, by using colored highlighters to signal connections between themes or ideas.
- For a new perspective on your research, try looking at your work while wearing each of Edward de Bono's six "thinking hats": the white hat (facts and figures), the red hat (emotions and feelings), the black hat (cautious and careful), the yellow hat (speculative-positive), the green hat (creative thinking), and the blue hat (control of thinking).[22]

- Ask colleagues from other disciplines to recommend work by the best and most accessible writers in their field. As you read, consider form as well as content: What strategies do these authors use to engage and inform their readers? Are those strategies different from the ones commonly used in your discipline? Can you spot any new techniques worth borrowing?

BECOMING A STYLISH WRITER

Disciplinary styles constantly shift and evolve: half a century from now, perhaps historians will have embraced personal pronouns and evolutionary biologists will have rejected them, rather than vice versa. Yet some principles of good writing remain timeless. In the preface, I note that all stylish academic writers hold three ideals in common: communication, craft, and creativity. *Communication* implies respect for one's audience; *craft,* respect for language; *creativity,* respect for academic endeavor. In closing, I would like to add three further Cs: concreteness, choice, and courage. *Concreteness* is a verbal technique; *choice,* an intellectual right; *courage,* a frame of mind. Together, these principles offer a flexible framework on which writers from different disciplines can drape a rich variety of words and texts.

Concrete language is the stylish writer's magic bullet, a verbal strategy so simple and powerful that I am amazed it is so seldom mentioned in academic writing handbooks. (Only 27 percent of the advanced guides in my one hundred–book sample even mention concrete language as a stylistic principle.) Whether in the title, summary statement, opening paragraph, or anywhere else in an academic article or book, just a few visual images or concrete examples—words that engage the senses and anchor your ideas in physical space—can combat the numbing sense of disorientation that most readers feel when confronted with too much abstraction. All of the stylish academic writers quoted in this book make liberal use of concrete language, whether to hook their readers' attention, to tell a story, or to explain theoretical concepts.

The principle of *choice,* however, means that you don't have to use concrete language if you don't want to. Throughout this book, I present stylish writing as a series of considered decisions: no choice is intrinsically "right" or "wrong," but each decision you make will trigger different consequences and invite different responses from readers. For example, your choice to employ technical jargon may earn you kudos from peers within your own subdiscipline but could endanger your chances of winning a research grant awarded by a university-wide committee or multidisciplinary organization. Which matters to you more? Can you tailor two different pieces of writing to suit the two different audiences? Even more ambitiously, can you develop a writing style calculated to please and impress both groups? Stylish academic writers constantly engage in what educational researcher Donald Schön calls "reflective practice"; that is, they self-consciously monitor their own methods, principles, and choices, adjusting their way of working based on experience, feedback, and other forms of learning.[1]

Of course, making the choice to change one's writing style requires *courage,* especially for academics whose research careers are not yet well established. "My dissertation advisor wouldn't possibly allow me to use personal pronouns or metaphors," I have heard PhD students lament. A junior colleague recently confessed to me, "I'd like to try a more experimental structure for my next article, but until I get tenure, I can't afford to take the chance." But why always assume the worst rather than aim for the best? How will you know you are doomed to failure unless you give something a try? Virtually every successful academic researcher I know can tell stories both of rejection ("The referees hated it!") and eventual success ("so I sent it to a different journal, and it ended up winning a prize for the best article of the year"). Moreover, even PhD students are not always quite as powerless as they believe. "Here's an article by so-and-so, an eminent researcher in my field; I admire the way she structures her article, and I would like to try something similar with my literature review—what do you think?" Only an unusually close-minded and authoritarian supervisor (unfortunately, they do exist!) would refuse to even consider the question.

And so I end this book with the following exhortation to new and experienced academics alike: stretch your mind by stretching your writing; don't be afraid to try new things; and keep in mind that even a few small changes can make a big difference. Analyze the writing of colleagues you admire and identify just one or two new stylistic techniques to try. How do they capture and hold your attention, structure a sentence or a paragraph, explain a difficult concept, tell the story of their research, or acknowledge their colleagues? In his influential book *Scholarship Reconsidered*, educational researcher Ernest Boyer notes that "the work of the professor becomes consequential only as it is understood by others."[2] If you resolve to model your own scholarship on work that *you* find consequential—writing that engages, impresses, and inspires—you will already be well on your way to becoming a more stylish writer.

APPENDIX

Except for several examples in the "Things to Try" sections (which I wrote myself), all unreferenced quotations in this book come from a corpus of one thousand recent articles drawn from peer-reviewed journals in ten academic disciplines across the sciences, social sciences, and humanities (one hundred articles per discipline). The articles appeared in the volumes/issues listed below. Out of courtesy for authors whose work is unfavorably cited, I have not disclosed full citation information here (except in one case where I was required to do so for copyright reasons). However, all of the articles in the corpus are available electronically and can be located via an Internet search.

For eight of the ten disciplines, I selected the twenty most recent articles from each of five different journals. The two exceptions are in psychology, where I chose the five most recent articles from each of twenty journals, and higher education, where I chose the fifty most recent articles from a single journal *(Studies in Higher Education)* and ten articles each from five additional journals. In each of the ten disciplines surveyed, the journals were chosen to represent a broad cross section of well-regarded peer-reviewed publications, based both on peer recommendations and objective measures of peer esteem. As a general rule, I opted for journals with high impact factors (where such ratings were available) and took care to include publications from a range of international locations. However, it is important to note that no given set of five journals from a single discipline—or even from twenty journals, as with my psychology sample—can be considered fully representative. Academics invariably have their own, sometimes idiosyncratic, lists of "the most important journals" in their fields or subfields. My data set provides a selective snapshot of disciplinary scholarship in the early twenty-first century, not a definitive panorama of the infinitely complex and varied landscape of academic endeavor.

Discipline	Journals and Volume/Issues (2006–2008)
Medicine	*Annals of Internal Medicine* 147 (6–12) *Internal Medicine Journal* 37 (9–12) *Journal of the American Medical Association* 298 (18–24) *The Lancet* 370 (9598–9604) *New England Journal of Medicine* 357 (22–26)
Evolutionary Biology	*The American Naturalist* 169 (2–4) *Evolution* 61 (1–2) *Molecular Biology and Evolution* 24 (1–2) *Proceedings of the Royal Society B: Biological Sciences* 274 (1606–1607) *Systematic Biology* 56 (1–2)
Computer Science	*ACM Transactions on Database Systems* 32 (2–4) *ACM Transactions on Information Systems* 24 (4), 25 (1–4) *Acta Informatica* 44 (1–8) *Aslib Proceedings* 59 (3–6) *Journal of Research and Practice in Information Technology* 39 (1–4)
Higher Education	*Higher Education* 52 (3–4) *Journal of Higher Education* 78 (3–5) *Research in Higher Education* 47 (6–8) *Review of Higher Education* 29 (3–4), 30 (1) *Studies in Higher Education* 31 (3–6), 32 (1–4) *Teaching in Higher Education* 11 (3–4)

Psychology	*Behavioral and Brain Sciences* 30 (2–3), 31 (1) *Biological Psychology* 74 (1) *Child Development* 78 (1) *Clinical Psychology Review* 27 (1) *Counseling Psychologist* 35 (1–3) *Educational Psychologist* 42 (2) *Educational Psychology Review* 19 (1–2) *Journal of Abnormal Psychology* 116 (1) *Journal of Applied Psychology* 92 (1) *Journal of Child Psychology and Psychiatry* 48 (1) *Journal of Consulting and Clinical Psychology* 75 (1) *Journal of Counseling Psychology* 54 (1) *Journal of Personality and Social Psychology* 92 (1) *Journal of the American Academy of Child and Adolescent Psychiatry* 46 (1) *Journal of the Learning Sciences* 15 (4), 16 (1) *Psychological Bulletin* 133 (1) *Psychonomic Bulletin and Review* 14 (1) *Psychophysiology* 44 (1) *Psychotherapy and Psychosomatics* 76 (2) *Trends in Cognitive Sciences* 11 (1)
Anthropology	*American Antiquity* 72 (1–4), 73 (2) *Cultural Anthropology* 22 (4), 22 (1–4) *Current Anthropology* 48 (1–4), 49 (2) *Journal of Human Evolution* 50 (6), 52 (1–2) *Social Networks* 29 (1–3)
Law	*Australian and New Zealand Journal of Criminology* 39 (3), 40 (1–3) *Columbia Law Review* 107 (1–8) *Common Market Law Review* 44 (3–6) *Harvard Law Review* 119 (4–8), 120 (2–4, 6–8), 121 (2) *Journal of International Economic Law* 10 (3–4)
Philosophy	*Dialectica* 60 (4), 61 (2, 4), 62 (1) *Ethics* 117 (2–4), 118 (1–3)

(continued)

Discipline	Journals and Volume/Issues (2006–2008)
	Mind and Language 22 (3–5), 23 (1–3)
	Philosophy East and West 57 (1–4)
	The Review of Metaphysics 60 (4), 61 (1–4)
History	*American Historical Review* 112 (1–5), 113 (1–2)
	Isis 97 (4), 98 (1–4), 99 (1–2)
	Journal of the History of Ideas 68 (1–3), 69 (1)
	Journal of the History of Sexuality 16 (1–3), 17 (1–2)
	Modern Asian Studies 41 (1–3)
Literary Studies	*Critical Inquiry* 32 (4), 33 (1, 3), 34 (1)
	Eighteenth-Century Studies 39 (4), 40 (1–3)
	Modernism/Modernity 13 (2), 14 (1–2)
	PMLA 113 (2–3, 5), 114 (2–3, 5), 115 (2)
	Victorian Studies 49 (1–4), 50 (1)

COMMENTS ON CHAPTER 2

To generate the stylistic data and statistics graphed in Figures 2.1 and 2.2, I worked with a research assistant to analyze five hundred articles from the corpus described above: fifty articles from each discipline, using the ten most recent articles from each of the five journals surveyed. (For psychology, we used five articles each from ten journals; for higher education, we used ten articles each from every journal except *Teaching in Higher Education*.) We established precise criteria for each stylistic feature and frequently cross-checked each other's judgments.

For the statistics in Figure 2.1, we looked only at the first one thousand words of each article, not counting quotations and citations:

- *Personal pronouns* refer only to the first-person pronouns *I* and *we*, except where *we* is used impersonally ("from these results we surmised") rather than in reference to the authors ("we analyzed the data and found").

- *Unique or hybrid structure* means that the article has a structure that significantly diverges from the conventional IMRAD (Introduction, Method, Results, and Discussion) model and its variants.
- *Engaging title/engaging opening* indicates that the title or opening paragraph employs one or more of the following attention-getting strategies: a quotation, question, pun, anecdote, provocative statement, unusual turn of phrase, or literary device such as alliteration, metaphor, or wordplay.
- *Common abstract nouns* are nominalizations formed using any of the following suffixes: *-ance, -ence, -ity, -ness, -ion, -ment, -ism*.
- *Be verbs* include *is, am, was, were, are, be, been.*

For the citation statistics in Figure 2.2, we counted the number of items in the citation list for each article. Where a citation list did not exist, we counted the number of footnotes, not the full number of references cited.

COMMENTS ON CHAPTER 3

The bibliographic survey described in Chapter 3 was conducted by an undergraduate researcher, Louisa Shen, with the support of a ten-week summer research scholarship from the University of Auckland. Louisa describes her methodology as follows:

At the outset, I compiled a large Endnote Bibliography of more than 500 writing guide titles as a reference point. Next, I established seven disciplinary categories and chose 12 recent titles for each category (all published between 2000 and 2010) to make up 84 guides in total. I selected for analysis books aimed at graduate students and/ or established academic researchers. Where guides written exclusively for this demographic were not available, I chose books that targeted both undergraduates and postgraduates. If the guide did not indicate its intended audience, I made a judgment call on its "academic level" based on whether it dealt with writing for research and publication. No guides that were solely for undergraduates made my short list, even though such texts constitute most of the writing guides field. I then analyzed each selected guide for style and content and generated a report (on average 16–18 pages) for each of the seven disciplinary categories. I also produced a short summary of each guide for the annotated bibliography. The data was then collated into graphs to show trends, and I completed a percentage breakdown of the findings.

At a later stage, Louisa reclassified the writing guides into four overarching disciplinary categories—arts and humanities, science and engineering, social sciences (including business and economics), and generic—and added to her bibliography sixteen additional books, including several well-known writing guides that, while not necessarily aimed at advanced academic writers, might very likely be found on academics' bookshelves: for example, Strunk and White's *Elements of Style,* Zinsser's *On Writing Well,* Williams's *Style,* and Gowers's *The Complete Plain Words.* This brought the total number of writing guides to one hundred (twenty-five guides per category). The statistics quoted in Chapter 3 and elsewhere throughout this book refer to the full one hundred–guide sample.

NOTES

1. RULES OF ENGAGEMENT

1. William Strunk Jr. and E. B. White, *The Elements of Style,* 4th ed. (Needham Heights, MA: Allyn and Bacon, 2000), 66.

2. E. B. White, *Charlotte's Web* (London: Hamish Hamilton, 1952), 37–38.

3. Unless otherwise noted, all unattributed quotations come from my data set of one thousand academic articles, for which I provide a full list of journal names and volume numbers in the appendix.

4. John Swales, *Genre Analysis: English in Academic and Research Settings* (Cambridge: Cambridge University Press, 1990); Anna Duszak, ed., *Cultures and Styles of Academic Discourse* (Berlin and New York: Mouton de Gruyter, 1997); Tony Becher and Paul Trowler, *Academic Tribes and Territories: Intellectual Enquiry and the Culture of Disciplines,* 2nd rev. ed. (Philadelphia, PA: Open University Press, 2003); Marjorie Garber, *Academic Instincts* (Princeton, NJ: Princeton University Press, 2001); Jonathan Culler, "Bad Writing and Good Philosophy," in *Just Being Difficult? Academic Writing in the Public Arena,* ed. Jonathan Culler and Kevin Lamb (Stanford: Stanford University Press, 2003).

5. Ken Hyland, *Disciplinary Discourses: Social Interactions in Academic Writing* (Ann Arbor: University of Michigan Press, 2004), 40.

6. William Zinsser, *On Writing Well: An Informal Guide to Writing Nonfiction* (New York: Harper & Row, 1980), 5; Joseph M. Williams, *Style: Lessons in Clarity and Grace,* 9th ed. (New York: Pearson Longman, 2007), 221; Peter Elbow, *Writing with Power: Techniques for Mastering the Writing Process* (Oxford: Oxford University Press, 1981); Richard A. Lanham, *Revising Prose,* 3rd ed. (New York: Macmillan, 1992); Howard S. Becker, *Writing for Social Scientists: How to Start*

and Finish Your Thesis, Book, or Article, 2nd ed. (Chicago: Chicago University Press, 2007); Strunk and White, *Elements of Style,* xvi.

7. Patricia Nelson Limerick, "Dancing with Professors: The Trouble with Academic Prose," *New York Times Book Review,* October 31, 1993.

8. Ibid.

9. Strunk and White, *Elements of Style,* 66.

2. ON BEING DISCIPLINED

1. *Oxford English Dictionary,* 2nd ed., s.v. "discipline."

2. See Carolin Kreber, *The University and Its Disciplines: Teaching and Learning within and beyond Disciplinary Boundaries* (New York and London: Routledge, 2009), especially the chapters by Gary Poole ("Academic Disciplines: Homes or Barricades?"), David Pace ("Opening History's 'Black Boxes': Decoding the Disciplinary Unconscious of Historians"), and Paul Trowler ("Beyond Epistemological Essentialism: Academic Tribes in the Twenty-First Century").

3. Clark Kerr, *The Uses of the University* (Cambridge, MA: Harvard University Press, 1963), 20.

4. Andrew Abbott, *Chaos of Disciplines* (Chicago: University of Chicago Press, 2001), 11.

5. Lorenzo Amuso, "La Ferrari fa il pit stop in ospedale," *Il Giornale,* August 30, 2006.

6. Lee Shulman, "Signature Pedagogies in the Professions," *Daedalus* 134, no. 3 (Summer 2005): 52–59.

7. Russell Gray (psychology), John Hattie (education), Anne Salmond (anthropology), Brian Boyd (English).

8. Tony Becher and Paul Trowler, *Academic Tribes and Territories: Intellectual Enquiry and the Culture of Disciplines,* 2nd rev. ed. (Philadelphia, PA: Open University Press, 2003), 14.

9. Anthony Biglan, "Characteristics of Subject Matter in Different Academic Fields," *Journal of Applied Psychology* 57, no. 3 (1973): 195–203.

3. A GUIDE TO THE STYLE GUIDES

1. Paul Trowler, "Beyond Epistemological Essentialism: Academic Tribes in the Twenty-First Century," in *The University and Its Disciplines: Teaching and Learning within and beyond Disciplinary Boundaries,* ed. Carolin Kreber (New York: Routledge, 2009), 189.

2. Richard Marggraf Turley, *Writing Essays: A Guide for Students in English and the Humanities* (New York: Routledge, 2000), 6.

3. Lynn P. Nygaard, *Writing for Scholars: A Practical Guide to Making Sense and Being Heard* (Oslo, Norway: Universitetsforlaget, 2008), 36.

4. Howard S. Becker, *Writing for Social Scientists: How to Start and Finish Your Thesis, Book, or Article,* 2nd ed. (Chicago: University of Chicago Press, 2007).

5. Brian David Mogck, *Writing to Reason: A Companion for Philosophy Students and Instructors* (Oxford: Blackwell, 2008), 20.

6. Harold Rabinowitz and Suzanne Vogel, *The Manual of Scientific Style: A Guide for Authors, Editors, and Researchers* (Amsterdam and Boston: Academic Press, 2009), 6.

7. Bruce A. Thyer, *Preparing Research Articles* (Oxford and New York: Oxford University Press, 2008), 57.

8. Stephen J. Pyne, *Voice and Vision: A Guide to Writing History and Other Serious Non-Fiction* (Cambridge, MA: Harvard University Press, 2009), 140.

9. Pat Francis, *Inspiring Writing in Art and Design: Taking a Line for a Write* (Bristol, UK: Intellect, 2009).

10. Nygaard, *Writing for Scholars.*

11. Robert Goldbort, *Writing for Science* (New Haven, CT: Yale University Press, 2006).

12. Angela Thody, *Writing and Presenting Research* (London: Sage, 2006).

13. Becker, *Writing for Social Scientists.*

14. Stephen Brown, *Writing Marketing: Literary Lessons from Academic Authorities* (London: Sage, 2005), 182.

15. Peter J. Richerson and Robert Boyd, *Not by Genes Alone* (Chicago: University of Chicago Press, 2005), 116–121.

4. VOICE AND ECHO

Mermin Source: Nathaniel David Mermin, "Copenhagen Computation: How I Learned to Stop Worrying and Love Bohr," *IBM Journal of Research and Development* 48 (2004): 54, 56–57; "The Amazing Many-Colored Relativity Engine," *American Journal of Physics* 56 (1988): 600; "From Cbits to Qbits: Teaching Computer Scientists Quantum Mechanics," *American Journal of Physics* 71 (2003): 23.

Heilbron Source: John L. Heilbron, "Bohr's First Theories of the Atom," *Physics Today* 38, no. 10 (1985): 28; *The Sun in the Church: Cathedrals as Solar Observatories* (Cambridge, MA: Harvard University Press, 1999), 225.

Behar Source: Ruth Behar, "Dare We Say 'I'?" *Chronicle of Higher Education* 40, no. 43 (1994): B2; *The Vulnerable Observer: Anthropology That Breaks Your Heart* (Boston: Beacon, 1996), 177.

1. American Psychological Association, *The Publication Manual of the American Psychological Association*, 2nd ed. (Washington, DC: American Psychological Association, 1974), 26. The first edition of the APA guide (1952) does not mention pronoun usage at all; subsequent revisions (1957 and 1967) encourage the impersonal passive voice.

2. *The ACS Style Guide: Effective Communication of Scientific Information*, 3rd ed. (Oxford: Oxford University Press, 2006), 43–44; American Medical Association, *AMA Manual of Style: A Guide for Authors and Editors*, 10th ed. (Oxford: Oxford University Press, 2007), 315; Council of Science Editors, *Scientific Style and Format: The CSE Manual for Authors, Editors, and Publishers*, 7th ed. (Reston, VA: Council of Science Editors, 2006), 82.

3. Peter Elbow, *Writing with Power: Techniques for Mastering the Writing Process* (Oxford: Oxford University Press, 1981), 351.

5. SMART SENTENCING

Beer Source: Gillian Beer, *Darwin's Plots: Evolutionary Narrative in Darwin, George Eliot and Nineteenth Century Fiction* (London: Routledge and Kegan Paul, 1983), 3–4.

Salmond Source: Anne Salmond, "Their Body Is Different, Our Body Is Different: European and Tahitian Navigators in the 18th Century," *History and Anthropology* 16, no. 2 (2005): 171, 169, 183.

Webster Source: James Webster, *Haydn's "Farewell" Symphony and the Idea of Classical Style: Through-Composition and Cyclic Integration in His Instrumental Music* (Cambridge: Cambridge University Press, 1991), 334, 275, 1; "Music, Pathology, Sexuality, Beethoven, Schubert," *Nineteenth-Century Music* 17, vol. 1 (1993): 89.

1. Richard A. Lanham, *Revising Prose*, 3rd ed. (New York: Macmillan, 1992). Lanham phrases the question as "Who's kicking who?"

2. Kwame Anthony Appiah, *Cosmopolitanism: Ethics in a World of Strangers* (New York: Norton, 2006), xi.

3. Daniel C. Dennett, "Who's on First? Heterophenomenology Explained," *Journal of Consciousness Studies* 10, nos. 9–10 (2003): 1.

4. Brian Boyd, "Art and Evolution: Spiegelman's *The Narrative Corpse*," *Philosophy and Literature* 32, no. 1 (2008): 31.

5. Anne Salmond, "Their Body Is Different, Our Body Is Different: European and Tahitian Navigators in the 18th Century," *History and Anthropology* 16, no. 2 (2005): 168.

6. Michèle Lamont, *How Professors Think: Inside the Curious World of Academic Judgment* (Cambridge, MA: Harvard University Press, 2009), 64–65.

7. Charles McGrath, "J. D. Salinger, Author Who Fled Fame, Dies at 91 (Obituary)," *New York Times,* January 29, 2010.

8. See also Helen Sword, *The Writer's Diet* (New Zealand: Pearson Education, 2007).

6. TEMPTING TITLES

Sacks Source: Oliver Sacks, "The Power of Music," *Brain* 129, no. 10 (2006): 2529; Anatole Broyard, "Good Books Abut (sic) Being Sick," *New York Times,* April 1, 1990. See also Sacks, *Awakenings* (New York: Doubleday, 1973); *The Man Who Mistook His Wife for a Hat and Other Clinical Tales* (New York: Simon and Schuster, 1998); *An Anthropologist on Mars: Seven Paradoxical Tales* (New York: Knopf, 1995); *Musicophilia: Tales of Music and the Brain* (New York: Knopf, 2007); *The Island of the Colorblind* (New York: Vintage, 1997); *A Leg to Stand On* (New York: Touchstone Books, 1984); and *Uncle Tungsten: Memories of a Chemical Boyhood* (New York: Knopf, 2001).

Altemeyer Source: Bob Altemeyer, "What Happens When Authoritarians Inherit the Earth? A Simulation," *Analyses of Social Issues and Public Policy* 3, no. 1 (2003): 161–169; "Why Do Religious Fundamentalists Tend to Be Prejudiced?" *International Journal for the Psychology of Religion* 13, no. 1 (2003): 17–28. See also Bob Altemeyer and Bruce Hunsberger, "A Revised Religious Fundamentalism Scale: The Short and Sweet of It," *International Journal for the Psychology of Religion* 14, no. 1 (2004): 47–54.

Wadler Source: P. Wadler and R. B. Findler, "Well-Typed Programs Can't Be Blamed," paper presented at the European Symposium on Programming (ESOP), Budapest, Hungary, 2008; S. Marlow and S. P. Jones, "Making a Fast Curry: Push/Enter vs. Eval/Apply for Higher-Order Languages," *Journal of Functional Programming* 16, nos. 4–5 (2006): 415–449; R. Lämmel and S. P. Jones, "Scrap Your Boilerplate: A Practical Design Pattern for Generic Programming," *ACM SIGPLAN Notices* 38, no. 3 (2003): 26–37; Philip Wadler, "Et tu, XML? The Downfall of the Relational Empire," paper presented at the 27th

Annual Conference on Very Large Databases (VLDB), Rome, Italy, 2001; M. Odersky, E. Runne, and P. Wadler, "Two Ways to Bake Your Pizza: Translating Parameterised Types into Java," paper presented at the International Seminar on Generic Programming, Germany, 2000; S. Lindley, P. Wadler, and J. Yallop, "Idioms Are Oblivious, Arrows Are Meticulous, Monads Are Promiscuous," paper presented at the Mathematically Structured Functional Programming workshop, Iceland, 2008.

1. Margaret Henley, "'Throwing a Sheep' at Marshall McLuhan," Tertiary Education Research in New Zealand (TERNZ) Conference, Auckland, November 2007. Retrieved June 24, 2009, from http://www.herdsa.org.nz/Ternz/2007/abstracts_all1.htm#henley.

2. Gérard Genette, *Paratexts: Thresholds of Interpretation,* trans. J. Lewin (Cambridge: Cambridge University Press, 1997).

3. Richard Dawkins, *The Selfish Gene* (Oxford: Oxford University Press, 1976); *The Blind Watchmaker* (Harlow, UK: Longman Scientific and Technical, 1986); *Climbing Mount Improbable* (London: Viking, 1996).

4. Richard Dawkins, "Bees Are Easily Distracted," *Science* 165, no. 3895 (1969): 751.

5. G. A. Pearson, ed., *Why Children Die: A Pilot Study* (London: CEMACH, 2006).

6. James Hartley, "To Attract or to Inform?" *Journal of Technical Writing and Communication* 35, no. 2 (2005): 207.

7. The bar for admission to the "engaging and informative" category was very low: I classified as "engaging" any title whose author appeared to have consciously made even the most modest attempt to amuse, entertain, or capture the attention of the intended audience—for example, by asking a question, using a metaphor, or making a provocative statement.

8. Marjorie Garber, *Academic Instincts* (Princeton, NJ: Princeton University Press, 2001), 33.

7. HOOKS AND SINKERS

Ameratunga Source: Shanthi Ameratunga, Martha Hijar, and Robyn Norton, "Road-Traffic Injuries: Confronting Disparities to Address a Global Health Problem," *The Lancet* 367, no. 9521 (2006): 1533.

Dawkins Source: Richard Dawkins, *Climbing Mount Improbable* (London: Viking, 1996), 1.

Greenblatt Source: Stephen Greenblatt, "Racial Memory and Literary History," *PMLA* 116, no. 1 (2001): 48; "Writing as Performance: Revealing 'The Calculation That Underlies the Appearance of Effortlessness,'" *Harvard Magazine*, September/October 2007, 45.

1. Hunter S. Thompson, *Fear and Loathing in Las Vegas: A Savage Journey to the Heart of the American Dream* (London: Flamingo, 1993), 3.

2. John Swales, *Genre Analysis: English in Academic Research Settings* (Cambridge: Cambridge University Press, 1990).

3. Jonathan Wolff, "Literary Boredom," *Guardian*, September 24, 2007.

4. Stephen Greenblatt, "Writing as Performance: Revealing 'The Calculation That Underlies the Appearance of Effortlessness,'" *Harvard Magazine*, September/October 2007, 45.

8. THE STORY NET

Denning Source: *Hinz v. Berry* [1970] 2 QB 40 at 42; *Beswick v. Beswick* [1966] Ch. 538; *Cummings v. Granger* [1977] 1 All E.R. 104, 106; *Miller v. Jackson* [1977] QB 966.

Banes Source: Sally Banes, "Choreographing Community: Dancing in the Kitchen," *Dance Chronicle* 25, no. 1 (2002): 143; "Olfactory Performances," *Drama Review* 45, no. 1 (2001): 69–70.

Clough Source: Peter Clough, *Narrative and Fictions in Educational Research* (Buckingham: Open University Press, 2002): 17, 25; "'Again Fathers and Sons': The Mutual Construction of Self, Story, and Special Educational Needs," *Disability and Society* 11, no. 1 (1996): 72–73, 81; "Theft and Ethics in Life Portrayal: Lolly—The Final Story," *International Journal of Qualitative Studies in Education (QSE)* 17, no. 3 (2004): 376.

1. Brian Boyd, *On the Origin of Stories: Evolution, Cognition, and Fiction* (Cambridge, MA: Harvard University Press, 2009).

2. See, for example: Ruth Behar, *The Vulnerable Observer: Anthropology That Breaks Your Heart* (Boston: Beacon, 1996); Clifford Geertz, *Works and Lives: The Anthropologist as Author* (Stanford: Stanford University Press, 1988); Roberto Franzosi, "Narrative Analysis—Or Why (and How) Sociologists Should Be Interested in Narrative," *Annual Review of Sociology* 24 (1998): 517–554; Peter Clough, *Narrative and Fictions in Educational Research* (Buckingham: Open University Press, 2002); Robert J. Nash, *Liberating Scholarly Writing: The Power*

of Personal Narrative (New York: Teachers College Press, 2004); Robert J. Pelias, *A Methodology of the Heart* (Walnut Creek, CA: AltaMira Press, 2004); Richard Delgado, "Storytelling for Oppositionists and Others: A Plea for Narrative," *Michigan Law Review* 87, no. 8 (1989): 2411–2441; Barbara Czarniawska-Joerges, *Narrating the Organization: Dramas of Institutional Identity* (Chicago: University of Chicago Press, 1997); Rita Charon, "Narrative and Medicine," *New England Journal of Medicine* 350 (2004): 862–864.

3. Judith Pascoe, *The Sarah Siddons Audio Files: Romanticism and the Lost Voice* (Ann Arbor: University of Michigan Press, 2011).

4. E. M. Forster, *Aspects of the Novel* (London: Edward Arnold, 1974), 60.

5. Quoted in Robert S. Root-Bernstein, "The Sciences and Arts Share a Common Creative Aesthetic," in *The Elusive Synthesis: Aesthetics and Science,* ed. Alfred I. Tauber (Dordrecht, Netherlands, and Boston: Kluwer, 1996), 67–68.

6. Bill Barton, *The Language of Mathematics: Telling Mathematical Tales* (New York: Springer, 2008), 1.

7. John L. Heilbron, *The Sun in the Church: Cathedrals as Solar Observatories* (Cambridge, MA: Harvard University Press, 1999), 289.

8. Tai Peseta, "Troubling Our Desires for Research and Writing within the Academic Development Project," *International Journal for Academic Development* 12, no. 1 (2007): 16.

9. Mark Twain, *The Adventures of Huckleberry Finn* (New York: C. L. Webster, 1885); Charles Dickens, *Oliver Twist* (London: Penguin, 1994); Edgar Allan Poe, *The Telltale Heart and Other Writings* (New York: Bantam Books, 2004); William Faulkner, *The Sound and the Fury* (New York: Norton, 1993); Agatha Christie, *The Murder of Roger Ackroyd: A Hercule Poirot Mystery* (New York: Black Dog and Leventhal, 1926).

9. SHOW AND TELL

Corballis Source: Michael C. Corballis, *From Hand to Mouth: The Origins of Language* (Princeton, NJ: Princeton University Press, 2002), 3–5.

Boyd Source: Brian Boyd and Robert Michael Pyle, *Nabokov's Butterflies: Unpublished and Uncollected Writings* (Boston: Beacon Press, 2000), 1–4, 17, 31.

Pinker Source: Steven Pinker, *Words and Rules: The Ingredients of Language* (London: Weidenfeld and Nicolson, 1999), xi.

1. Archibald MacLeish, "Ars Poetica," in *Collected Poems, 1917–1982* (Boston: Houghton Mifflin Company, 1985), 106.

2. Glyn W. Humphreys and M. Jane Riddoch, "How to Define an Object: Evidence from the Effects of Action on Perception and Attention," *Mind and Language* 22, no. 5 (2007): 543.

3. Steven Pinker, *Words and Rules: The Ingredients of Language* (London: Weidenfeld and Nicholson, 1999), 23.

4. Gillian Rose, "Family Photographs and Domestic Spacings: A Case Study," *Transactions of the Institute of British Geographers* 28, no. 1 (2003): 5–18; David Gegeo and Karen Ann Watson-Gegeo, "Whose Knowledge? Epistemological Collisions in Solomon Islands Community Development," *Contemporary Pacific* 14, no. 2 (2002): 379; Jeffrey Pfeffer and Tanya Menon, "Valuing Internal vs. External Knowledge: Explaining the Preference for Outsiders," *Management Science* 49, no. 2 (2003): 500.

5. Andrew C. Sparkes, "Embodiment, Academics, and the Audit Culture: A Story Seeking Consideration," *Qualitative Research* 7, no. 4 (2007): 522.

6. Howard Becker attributes the "hypothetical women impregnated by flying insects" example to ethicist Kathryn Pyne Addelson; the phrase "spherical cow," originally from a joke about theoretical physicists, is used by scientists to describe any highly simplified model of reality. Howard Becker, *Writing for Social Scientists: How to Start and Finish Your Thesis, Book, or Article,* 2nd ed. (Chicago: University of Chicago Press, 2007), 84; John Harte, *Consider a Spherical Cow: A Course in Environmental Problem Solving* (Sausalito, CA: University Science Books, 1988).

7. George Lakoff and Mark Johnson, *Philosophy in the Flesh: The Embodied Mind and Its Challenge to Western Thought* (New York: Basic Books, 1999); George Lakoff and Mark Johnson, *Metaphors We Live By* (Chicago: University of Chicago Press, 1981).

8. Peter Brooks, *Reading for the Plot: Design and Intention in Narrative* (New York: Alfred A. Knopf, 1984), xv.

9. Robert J. Sternberg, *Cupid's Arrow: The Course of Love through Time* (Cambridge: Cambridge University Press, 1998), 9.

10. Steven Mailloux, *Disciplinary Identities: Rhetorical Paths of English, Speech, and Composition* (New York: Modern Languages Association, 2006), 64.

11. H. B. Cott, *Adaptive Coloration in Animals* (London: Metheun, 1940), 158–159.

12. Leigh Van Valen, "A New Evolutionary Law," *Evolutionary Theory* 1 (1973): 17–21; Lewis Carroll, *Alice's Adventures in Wonderland and Through the Looking Glass* (New York: Cosimo, 2010), 20.

13. F. H. C. Crick and L. E. Orgel, "Selfish DNA: The Ultimate Parasite," *Nature* 284, no. 5757 (April 17, 1980): 604. The phrase "junk DNA" was coined by Susumu Ohno in 1972.

14. Ruth Behar, *The Vulnerable Observer: Anthropology That Breaks Your Heart* (Boston: Beacon Press, 1996), 19.

15. Marjorie Garber, "Why Can't Young Scholars Write Their Second Books First?" *Journal of Scholarly Publishing* 36, no. 3 (2005): 130.

16. Allan Paivio, *Mental Representations: A Dual Coding Approach* (Oxford: Oxford University Press, 1984).

17. Douglas R. Hofstadter and David Moser, "To Err Is Human; To Study Error-Making Is Cognitive Science," *Michigan Quarterly Review* 27, no. 2 (1989): 185.

10. JARGONITIS

Garber Source: Marjorie Garber, *Academic Instincts* (Princeton, NJ: Princeton University Press, 2001), 113, 137–138, 144, 100–101, 99, 119.

Crang Source: Mike Crang, "The Hair in the Gate: Visuality and Geographical Knowledge," *Antipode* 35, no. 2 (2003): 238–239.

Foucault Source: Michel Foucault, *Discipline and Punish: The Birth of the Prison*, trans. Alan Sheridan (New York: Pantheon Books, 1977), 214.

1. *Oxford English Dictionary*, 2nd ed., s.v. "jargon"; *Merriam-Webster's Collegiate Dictionary*, 11th ed., 2003, s.v. "jargon."

2. Derek Attridge, "Arche-Jargon," *Qui Parle* 5, no. 1 (1991): 44.

3. Roland Barthes, *Criticism and Truth*, trans. and ed. Katherine Pilcher Keuneman (London: Althone Press, 1987), 52; *Critique et Vérité* (Paris: Éditions de Seuil, 1966), 34.

4. Jacques Derrida, *Glas*, trans. John P. Leavey Jr. and Richard Rand (Lincoln and London: University of Nebraska Press, 1986), 220; *Glas* (Paris: Éditions Galilée, 1974), 246.

5. George Orwell, "Politics and the English Language," in *All Art is Propaganda: Critical Essays*, ed. George Packer (Orlando, FL: Harcourt, 2008), 277.

6. Anne Knish [Arthur Davison Ficke] and Emanuel Morgan [Witter Bynner], *Spectra: A Book of Poetic Experiments* (New York: Mitchell

Kennerley, 1926); Alan Sokal, "A Physicist Experiments with Cultural Studies," *Lingua Franca* 4 (May 1996): 62–64; Sokal, "Transgressing the Boundaries: Towards a Transformative Hermeneutics of Quantum Gravity," *Social Text* 46/47 (Spring/Summer 1996): 217–252.

7. "The Postmodernism Generator," http://www.elsewhere.org/pomo/; "The SCIgen Computer," http://pdos.csail.mit.edu/scigen/; and "Chomskybot," http://www.rubberducky.org/cgi-bin/chomsky.pl (all accessed December 14, 2010).

8. Orwell, "Politics and the English Language," 282.

9. Ray Land and Siân Bayne, "Screen or Monitor? Issues of Surveillance and Disciplinary Power in Online Learning Environments," in *Education in Cyberspace*, ed. Ray Land and Siân Bayne (Abingdon, UK: RoutledgeFalmer, 2005), 167–169.

10. Peter Brooks, *Reading for the Plot: Design and Intention in Narrative* (New York: Alfred A. Knopf, 1984), 272.

11. Jacques Derrida, "Différance," in *Margins of Philosophy*, trans. Alan Bass (Chicago: University of Chicago Press, 1982), 3–27.

11. STRUCTURAL DESIGNS

Shankweiler Source: Donald Shankweiler, "Words to Meanings," *Scientific Studies of Reading* 3, no. 2 (1999): 113–127.

Connors and Lunsford Source: Robert J. Connors and Andrea Lunsford, "Frequency of Formal Errors in Current College Writing, or Ma and Pa Kettle Do Research," *College Composition and Communication* 39, no. 4 (1988): 395.

Rosner Source: Victoria Rosner, *Modernism and the Architecture of Private Life* (New York: Columbia University Press, 2005), 1–2.

1. Annie Dillard, *The Writing Life* (New York: Harper & Row, 1989), 4.

2. Bob Altemeyer, "Why Do Religious Fundamentalists Tend to Be Prejudiced?" *International Journal for the Psychology of Religion* 13, no. 1 (2003): 17–28; David E. Guest and Neil Conway, "Communicating the Psychological Contract: An Employer Perspective," *Human Resource Management Journal* 12, no. 2 (2002): 22–38.

3. Virginia Woolf, *To the Lighthouse: The Original Holograph Draft*, transcribed and ed. Susan Dick (London: Hogarth Press, 1982), 48.

4. Linda Brodkey, "Writing on the Bias," *College English* 56, no. 5 (September 1994): 527–547.

5. Peter Elbow, *Writing with Power: Techniques for Mastering the Writing Process* (Oxford: Oxford University Press, 1981).

6. Peter Elbow, "The Music of Form: Rethinking Organization in Writing," *College Composition and Communication* 57, no. 4 (2006): 654–655.

7. Robert Pogue Harrison, *Forests: The Shadow of Civilization* (Chicago: University of Chicago Press, 1992).

8. David Ulansey, *The Origins of the Mithraic Mysteries: Cosmology and Salvation in the Ancient World* (Oxford: Oxford University Press, 1989), ix.

9. Douglas R. Hofstadter, *Metamagical Themas: Questing for the Essence of Mind and Pattern* (New York: Basic Books, 1985), vi.

12. POINTS OF REFERENCE

Goodrich Source: Peter Goodrich, "Satirical Legal Studies: From the Legists to the Lizard," *Michigan Law Review* 103, no. 3 (2004): 397, 402.

Grafton Source: Anthony Grafton, *The Footnote: A Curious History* (Cambridge, MA: Harvard University Press, 1997), 5–7, 9, 24.

1. Frances Kelly, "Writing in the Frame Lock," paper presented at the Writing Research across Borders Conference, Santa Barbara, CA, February 2008.

2. Robert Madigan, Susan Johnson, and Patricia Linton, "The Language of Psychology: APA Style as Epistemology," *American Psychologist* 4, no. 6 (1995): 428–434.

3. Robert J. Connors, "The Rhetoric of Citation Systems, Part II: Competing Epistemic Values in Citation," *Rhetoric Review* 17, no. 2 (1999): 239; Charles Bernstein, "Frame Lock," *College Literature* 21, no. 2 (1994): 119.

4. Connors, "Rhetoric of Citation Systems," 242; Bernstein, "Frame Lock," 119.

5. Quoted in Marjorie Garber, *Academic Instincts* (Princeton, NJ: Princeton University Press, 2001), 39.

6. Laurel Richardson, "Writing Strategies: Reaching Diverse Audiences," *Qualitative Research Methods* 21 (1990): 16; Connors "Rhetoric of Citation Systems," 222.

7. Vladimir Nabokov, *Pale Fire* (New York: Random House, 1989).

8. Michael C. Corballis, *From Hand to Mouth: The Origins of Language* (Princeton, NJ: Princeton University Press, 2002), 213.

9. Ted Cohen, "Identifying with Metaphor: Metaphors of Personal Identification," *Journal of Aesthetics and Art Criticism* 57, no. 4 (1999): 204.

10. "Common Law Origins of the Infield Fly Rule," *University of Pennsylvania Law Review* 123, no. 6 (1975): 1474–1481.

11. Anthony Grafton, *The Footnote: A Curious History* (Cambridge, MA: Harvard University Press, 1997), 6, 229.

12. Madigan, Johnson, and Linton, "Language of Psychology," 428–429.

13. Steve Wise, "Revolution in References: Give Readers a Chance by Putting Page Numbers," *Nature* 408, no. 204 (November 23, 2000): 402; David Henige, "Discouraging Verification: Citation Practices across the Disciplines," *Journal of Scholarly Publishing* 37, no. 2 (2006): 99–118; Stephen K. Donovan, "Comment: 'Discouraging Verification: Citation Practices across the Disciplines,'" *Journal of Scholarly Publishing* 37, no. 4 (2006): 313–316.

14. Henige, "Discouraging Verification," 107, 103.

15. Ken Hyland, *Disciplinary Discourses: Social Interactions in Academic Writing* (Ann Arbor: University of Michigan Press, 2004), 37.

16. Ken Hyland, "Humble Servants of the Discipline? Self-Mention in Research Articles," *English for Specific Purposes* 20, no. 3 (2001): 207–226.

13. THE BIG PICTURE

Coulthard Source: Malcolm Coulthard, "Author Identification, Idiolect, and Linguistic Uniqueness," *Applied Linguistics* 25, no. 4 (2004): 431, 445.

Donovan Source: Stephen K. Donovan, "Research Journals: Toward Uniformity or Retaining Diversity?" *Journal of Scholarly Publishing* 37, no. 3 (April 2006): 230; *Jamaican Rock Stars, 1823–1971: The Geologists Who Explored Jamaica* (Boulder, CO: Geological Society of America, 2010).

Culler Source: Jonathan Culler, "Bad Writing and Good Philosophy," in *Just Being Difficult? Academic Writing in the Public Arena*, ed. Jonathan Culler and Kevin Lamb (Stanford: Stanford University Press, 2003), 43, 47, 49.

1. Sally Banes, "Olfactory Performances," *Drama Review* 45, no. 1 (2001): 68, 74.

2. Thomas Carnahan and Sam McFarland, "Revisiting the Stanford Prison Experiment: Could Participant Self-Selection Have Led to the Cruelty?" *Personality and Social Psychology Bulletin* 33, no. 5 (2007): 603.

3. Ken Hyland, *Disciplinary Discourses: Social Interactions in Academic Writing,* (Ann Arbor: University of Michigan Press, 2004), 68–84.

4. *Oxford English Dictionary,* 2nd ed., s.v. "persuasion."

5. Ken Norris, Adrian Freeman, and Julian F. V. Vincent, "The Economics of Getting High: Decisions Made by Common Gulls Dropping Their Cockles to Open Them," *Behaviour* 137, no. 6 (2000): 785.

6. David Green, "New Academics' Perceptions of the Language of Teaching and Learning: Identifying and Overcoming Linguistic Barriers," *International Journal for Academic Development* 14, no. 1 (2009): 43.

7. Peter Brooks, *Reading for the Plot: Design and Intention in Narrative* (New York: Alfred A. Knopf, 1984), xi.

8. E. Ann Kaplan, *Trauma Culture: The Politics of Terror and Loss in Media and Literature* (New Brunswick, NJ: Rutgers University Press, 2005), 1.

9. Michael Corballis, *From Hand to Mouth: The Origins of Language* (Princeton, NJ: Princeton University Press, 2002), viii.

10. Charles Bernstein, "Frame Lock," *College Literature* 20, no. 2 (1994): 120–121.

11. Richard Dawkins, *Climbing Mount Improbable* (London: Viking, 1996), viii.

14. THE CREATIVE TOUCH

Grey and Sinclair Source: Christopher Grey and Amanda Sinclair, "Writing Differently," *Organization* 13, no. 3 (2006): 443–453.

Hofstadter Source: Douglas R. Hofstadter, *Gödel, Escher, Bach: An Eternal Golden Braid,* 20th anniv. ed. (New York: Basic Books, 1999), P-12, P-1, vi–vii, 27, xxi.

Dennett Source: Daniel Dennett, "The Part of Cognitive Science That Is Philosophy," *Topics in Cognitive Science* 1 (2009): 231–232.

1. Willa Cather, "Katherine Mansfield," in *Willa Cather on Writing: Critical Studies on Writing as an Art* (New York: Bison Books, 1988), 107–108.

2. David Welchman Gegeo, "Cultural Rapture and Indigeneity: The Challenge of (Re)visioning 'Place' in the Pacific," *Contemporary Pacific* 13, no. 2 (2001): 491–492. Italics in the original.

3. Bronwyn Davies, "The (Im)possibility of Intellectual Work in Neo-liberal Regimes," *Discourse: Studies in the Cultural Politics of Education* 26, no. 1 (2005): 2.

4. C. C. Diamond and Clay Shirky, "Health Information Technology: A Few Years of Magical Thinking?" *Health Affairs* 27, no. 5 (2008): 383.

5. Ladislav Kováč, "Science and September 11th: A Lesson in Relevance," *World Futures: The Journal of General Evolution* 59, no. 5 (2003): 319–320.

6. Roland Barthes, *The Pleasure of the Text,* trans. Richard Miller (New York: Hill and Wang, 1975), 4.

7. Douglas R. Hofstadter, *Gödel, Escher, Bach: An Eternal Golden Braid,* 20th anniv. ed. (New York: Basic Books, 1999), xxi, 364.

8. Martin Gardner, *The Ambidextrous Universe* (London: Penguin, 1967), 13.

9. *Oxford English Dictionary,* 2nd ed., s.v. "elegance."

10. J. D. Watson and F. H. C. Crick, "A Structure for Deoxyribose Nucleic Acid," *Nature* 171, no. 4356 (April 25, 1953): 737.

11. Selina Tusitala Marsh, "Theory 'versus' Pacific Island Writing: Toward a Tama'ita'i Criticism in the Works of Three Pacific Island Woman Poets," in *Inside Out: Literature, Cultural Politics, and Identity in the New Pacific,* ed. Vilsoni Hereniko and Rob Wilson (Lanham, MD: Rowman and Littlefield, 1999), 338; Cynthia B. Dillard, "Walking Ourselves Back Home: The Education of Teachers with/in the World," *Journal of Teacher Education* 53, no. 5 (2002).

12. Julian F. V. Vincent, "If It's Tanned It Must Be Dry: A Critique," *Journal of Adhesion* 85, no. 11 (2009): 768.

13. John L. Heilbron, *The Sun in the Church: Cathedrals as Solar Observatories* (Cambridge, MA: Harvard University Press, 1999), 288.

14. M. A. Rosanoff, "Edison in His Laboratory," *Harper's Monthly Magazine,* vol. 165, June/November 1932, 406.

15. For some suggestions on facilitating creative-critical interchanges in academic writing, see Peter Elbow, *Writing with Power: Techniques for Mastering the Writing Process* (Oxford: Oxford University Press, 1981); Rob Pope, *Textual Intervention: Critical and Creative Strategies for Literary Studies* (London: Routledge, 1995); and Linda Brodkey, *Writing Permitted in Designated Areas Only* (Minneapolis: University of Minnesota Press, 1996). On creative-critical modes in advanced research writing, see Stephen Brown, *Writing Marketing: Literary Lessons from Academic Authorities* (London: Sage, 2005); Frank L. Cioffi, *The Imaginative*

Argument: A Practical Manifesto for Writers (Princeton, NJ: Princeton University Press, 2005); Angela Thody, *Writing and Presenting Research* (London: Sage Publications, 2006); and Stephen J. Pyne, *Voice and Vision: A Guide to Writing History and Other Serious Non-fiction* (Cambridge, MA: Harvard University Press, 2009).

16. Richard Dawkins, *Climbing Mount Improbable* (London: Viking, 1996); Robert J. Sternberg, *Cupid's Arrow: The Course of Love through Time* (Cambridge: Cambridge University Press, 1998); Marjorie Garber, *Academic Instincts* (Princeton, NJ: Princeton University Press, 2001); Michael Corballis, *From Hand to Mouth: The Origins of Language* (Princeton, NJ: Princeton University Press, 2002); Ruth Behar, *The Vulnerable Observer: Anthropology That Breaks Your Heart* (Boston: Beacon Press, 1996).

17. See, for example, Edward de Bono, *Lateral Thinking: Creativity Step by Step* (New York: Harper Colophon, 1973); Richard Wiseman, *Did You Spot the Gorilla? How to Recognise the Hidden Opportunities in Your Life* (London: Arrow Books, 2004).

18. Dr. Seuss, "The Zax," in *The Sneetches and Other Stories* (London: Collins, 1984), 26–35.

19. Philip Pullman, "From Exeter to Jordan," *Oxford Today: The University Magazine* 14, no. 3 (Trinity 2002), 3.

20. Elbow, *Writing with Power.*

21. Tony Buzan, *The Mind Map Book: How to Use Radiant Thinking to Maximize Your Brain's Untapped Potential* (New York: Plume, 1996).

22. Edward de Bono, *Six Thinking Hats* (New York: Little, Brown, 1985).

AFTERWORD: BECOMING A STYLISH WRITER

1. Donald A. Schön, *The Reflective Practitioner: How Professionals Think in Action* (New York: Basic Books, 1984).

2. Ernest Boyer, *Scholarship Reconsidered: Priorities for the Professoriate* (Princeton, NJ: Carnegie Foundation for the Advancement of Teaching, 1990), 23.

BIBLIOGRAPHY

Abbott, Andrew. *Chaos of Disciplines*. Chicago: University of Chicago Press, 2001.

Altemeyer, Bob. "What Happens When Authoritarians Inherit the Earth? A Simulation." *Analyses of Social Issues and Public Policy* 3, no. 1 (2003): 161–169.

———. "Why Do Religious Fundamentalists Tend to Be Prejudiced?" *International Journal for the Psychology of Religion* 13, no. 1 (2003): 17–28.

Altemeyer, Bob, and Bruce Hunsberger. "A Revised Religious Fundamentalism Scale: The Short and Sweet of It." *International Journal for the Psychology of Religion* 14, no. 1 (2004): 47–54.

Ameratunga, Shanthi, Martha Hijar, and Robyn Norton. "Road-Traffic Injuries: Confronting Disparities to Address a Global Health Problem." *Lancet* 367, no. 9521 (2006): 1533–1540.

American Chemical Society. *The ACS Style Guide: Effective Communication of Scientific Information*. 3rd ed. Oxford: Oxford University Press, 2006.

American Medical Association. *AMA Manual of Style: A Guide for Authors and Editors*. 10th ed. Oxford: Oxford University Press, 2007.

American Psychological Association. *The Publication Manual of the American Psychological Association*. rev. ed. Washington, DC: American Psychological Association, 1952.

———. *The Publication Manual of the American Psychological Association*. rev. ed. Washington, DC: American Psychological Association, 1967.

——. *The Publication Manual of the American Psychological Association.* 2nd ed. Washington, DC: American Psychological Association, 1974.

Amuso, Lorenzo. "La Ferrari fa il pit stop in ospedale." *Il Giornale,* August 30, 2006.

Appiah, Kwame Anthony. *Cosmopolitanism: Ethics in a World of Strangers.* New York: Norton, 2006.

Attridge, Derek. "Arche-Jargon." *Qui Parle 5,* no. 1 (1991): 41–52.

Banes, Sally. "Choreographing Community: Dancing in the Kitchen." *Dance Chronicle 25,* no. 1 (2002): 143–161.

——. "Olfactory Performances." *Drama Review 45,* no. 1 (2001): 68–79.

Barthes, Roland. *Critique et Vérité.* Paris: Éditions de Seuil, 1966. Translated and edited by Katrine Pilcher Keuneman as *Criticism and Truth* (London: Athlone Press, 1987).

——. *The Pleasure of the Text.* Translated by Richard Miller. New York: Hill and Wang, 1975.

Barton, Bill. *The Language of Mathematics: Telling Mathematical Tales.* Vol. 44 of *Mathematics Education Library.* New York: Springer, 2008.

Becher, Tony, and Paul Trowler. *Academic Tribes and Territories: Intellectual Enquiry and the Culture of Disciplines.* 2nd rev. ed. Philadelphia, PA: Open University Press, 2003.

Becker, Howard S. *Writing for Social Scientists: How to Start and Finish Your Thesis, Book, or Article.* 2nd ed. Chicago: Chicago University Press, 2007.

Beer, Gillian. *Darwin's Plots: Evolutionary Narrative in Darwin, George Eliot and Nineteenth Century Fiction.* London: Routledge and Kegan Paul, 1983.

Behar, Ruth. "Dare We Say 'I'?" *Chronicle of Higher Education 40,* no. 43 (1994): B1–B2.

——. *The Vulnerable Observer: Anthropology That Breaks Your Heart.* Boston: Beacon Press, 1996.

Bernstein, Charles. "Frame Lock." *College Literature 21,* no. 2 (1994): 119–126.

Biglan, Anthony. "Characteristics of Subject Matter in Different Academic Fields." *Journal of Applied Psychology 57,* no. 3 (1973): 195–203.

Boyd, Brian. "Art and Evolution: Spiegelman's *The Narrative Corpse.*" *Philosophy and Literature 32,* no. 1 (2008): 31–57.

——. *On the Origin of Stories: Evolution, Cognition, and Fiction.* Cambridge, MA: Harvard University Press, 2009.

Boyd, Brian, and Robert Michael Pyle. *Nabokov's Butterflies: Unpublished and Uncollected Writings*. Boston: Beacon Press, 2000.

Boyer, Ernest. *Scholarship Reconsidered: Priorities for the Professoriate*. Princeton, NJ: Carnegie Foundation for the Advancement of Teaching, 1990.

Brodkey, Linda. "Writing on the Bias." *College English* 56, no. 5 (1994): 527–547.

———. *Writing Permitted in Designated Areas Only*. Minneapolis, MN: University of Minneapolis Press, 1996.

Brooks, Peter. *Reading for the Plot: Design and Intention in Narrative*. New York: Alfred A. Knopf, 1984.

Brown, Stephen. *Writing Marketing: Literary Lessons from Academic Authorities*. London: Sage, 2005.

Broyard, Anatole. "Good Books Abut [*sic*] Being Sick." *New York Times*, April 1, 1990. http://www.nytimes.com/1990/04/01/books/good-books-abut-being-sick.html.

Buzan, Tony. *The Mind Map Book: How to Use Radiant Thinking to Maximize Your Brain's Untapped Potential*. New York: Plume, 1996.

Carnahan, Thomas, and Sam McFarland. "Revisiting the Stanford Prison Experiment: Could Participant Self-Selection Have Led to the Cruelty?" *Personality and Social Psychology Bulletin* 33, no. 5 (2007): 603–614.

Carroll, Lewis. *Alice's Adventures in Wonderland* and *Through the Looking Glass*. New York: Cosimo, 2010.

Cather, Willa. "Katherine Mansfield." In *Willa Cather on Writing: Critical Studies on Writing as an Art*, 105–120. New York: Bison Books, 1988.

Charon, Rita. "Narrative and Medicine." *New England Journal of Medicine* 350, no. 9 (2004): 862–864.

Christie, Agatha. *The Murder of Roger Ackroyd: A Hercule Poirot Mystery*. New York: Black Dog and Leventhal, 1926.

Cioffi, Frank L. *The Imaginative Argument: A Practical Manifesto for Writers*. Princeton, NJ: Princeton University Press, 2005.

Clough, Peter. "'Again Fathers and Sons': The Mutual Construction of Self, Story, and Special Educational Needs." *Disability and Society* 11, no. 1 (1996): 71–82.

———. *Narrative and Fictions in Educational Research*. Buckingham, UK: Open University Press, 2002.

———. "Theft and Ethics in Life Portrayal: Lolly—The Final Story." *International Journal of Qualitative Studies in Education (QSE)* 17, no. 3 (2004): 371–382.

Cohen, Ted. "Identifying with Metaphor: Metaphors of Personal Identification." *Journal of Aesthetics and Art Criticism* 57, no. 4 (1999): 399–409.

"Common-Law Origins of the Infield Fly Rule." *University of Pennsylvania Law Review* 123, no. 6 (1975): 1474–1481.

Connors, Robert J. "The Rhetoric of Citation Systems, Part II: Competing Epistemic Values in Citation." *Rhetoric Review* 17, no. 2 (1999): 219–245.

Connors, Robert J., and Andrea Lunsford. "Frequency of Formal Errors in Current College Writing, or Ma and Pa Kettle Do Research." *College Composition and Communication* 39, no. 4 (1988): 395–409.

Cooper, Ezra, and Philip Wadler. "A Located Lambda Calculus." Preprint, submitted April 2, 2008. http://homepages.inf.ed.ac.uk/wadler/topics/links.html#arrows-and-idioms.

Corballis, Michael C. *From Hand to Mouth: The Origins of Language.* Princeton, NJ: Princeton University Press, 2002.

Cott, H. B. *Adaptive Coloration in Animals.* London: Metheun, 1940.

Coulthard, Malcolm. "Author Identification, Idiolect, and Linguistic Uniqueness." *Applied Linguistics* 25, no. 4 (2004): 431–447.

Council of Science Editors. *Scientific Style and Format: The CSE Manual for Authors, Editors, and Publisher.* 7th ed. Reston, VA: Council of Science Editors, 2006.

Crang, Mike. "The Hair in the Gate: Visuality and Geographical Knowledge." *Antipode* 35, no. 2 (2003): 238–243.

Crick, F. H. C. and L. E. Orgel. "Selfish DNA: The Ultimate Parasite." *Nature* 284 (April 17, 1980): 604–607.

Culler, Jonathan. "Bad Writing and Good Philosophy." In *Just Being Difficult? Academic Writing in the Public Arena,* edited by Jonathan Culler and Kevin Lamb, 43–57. Stanford: Stanford University Press, 2003.

Czarniawska-Joerges, Barbara. *Narrating the Organization: Dramas of Institutional Identity.* Chicago: University of Chicago Press, 1997.

Davies, Bronwyn. "The (Im)possibility of Intellectual Work in Neoliberal Regimes." *Discourse: Studies in the Cultural Politics of Education* 26, no. 1 (2005): 1–14.

Dawkins, Richard. "Arresting Evidence." *Sciences* 38, no. 6 (1998): 20–25.

———. "Bees Are Easily Distracted." *Science* 165, no. 3895 (1969): 751.

———. *The Blind Watchmaker.* Harlow, UK: Longman Scientific and Technical, 1986.

———. *Climbing Mount Improbable.* London: Viking, 1996.

———. *The Extended Phenotype: The Gene as a Unit of Selection.* Oxford: W. H. Freeman, 1982.

———. *The Selfish Gene.* Oxford: Oxford University Press, 1976.

de Bono, Edward. *Lateral Thinking: Creativity Step by Step.* New York: Harper Colophon, 1973.

———. *Six Thinking Hats.* New York: Little, Brown, 1985.

Delgado, Richard. "Storytelling for Oppositionists and Others: A Plea for Narrative." *Michigan Law Review* 87, no. 8 (1989): 2411–2441.

Dennett, Daniel C. "The Part of Cognitive Science That Is Philosophy." *Topics in Cognitive Science* 1 (2009): 231–236.

———. "Who's on First? Heterophenomenology Explained." *Journal of Consciousness Studies* 10, nos. 9–10 (2003): 19–30.

Derrida, Jacques. "Différance." In *Margins of Philosophy,* translated by Alan Bass, 3–27. Chicago: University of Chicago Press, 1982.

———. *Glas.* Paris: Éditions Galilée, 1974. Translated by John P. Leavey Jr. and Richard Rand as *Glas.* Lincoln: University of Nebraska Press, 1986.

Diamond, Carol C., and Clay Shirky. "Health Information Technology: A Few Years of Magical Thinking?" *Health Affairs* 27, no. 5 (2008): 383–390.

Dickens, Charles. *Oliver Twist.* London: Penguin, 1994.

Dillard, Annie. *The Writing Life.* New York: Harper and Row, 1989.

Dillard, Cynthia B. "Walking Ourselves Back Home: The Education of Teachers with/in the World." *Journal of Teacher Education* 53, no. 5 (2002): 383–392.

Donovan, Stephen K. "Comment: 'Discouraging Verification: Citation Practices across the Disciplines.'" *Journal of Scholarly Publishing* 37, no. 4 (2006): 313–316.

———. *Jamaican Rock Stars, 1823–1971: The Geologists Who Explored Jamaica.* Boulder, CO: Geological Society of America, 2010.

———. "Research Journals: Toward Uniformity or Retaining Diversity?" *Journal of Scholarly Publishing* 37, no. 3 (2006): 230–235.

Duszak, Anna, ed. *Cultures and Styles of Academic Discourse.* Berlin: Mouton de Gruyter, 1997.

Elbow, Peter. "The Music of Form: Rethinking Organization in Writing." *College Composition and Communication* 57, no. 4 (2006): 620–666.

————. *Writing with Power: Techniques for Mastering the Writing Process.* Oxford: Oxford University Press, 1981.

Forster, E. M. *Aspects of the Novel.* London: Edward Arnold, 1974.

Foucault, Michel. *Discipline and Punish: The Birth of the Prison.* Translated by Alan Sheridan. New York: Pantheon Books, 1977.

Francis, Pat. *Inspiring Writing in Art and Design: Taking a Line for a Write.* Bristol, UK: Intellect, 2009.

Franzosi, Roberto. "Narrative Analysis—or Why (and How) Sociologists Should Be Interested in Narrative." *Annual Review of Sociology* 24, no. 1 (1998): 517–554.

Garber, Marjorie. *Academic Instincts.* Princeton, NJ: Princeton University Press, 2001.

————. "Why Can't Young Scholars Write Their Second Books First?" *Journal of Scholarly Publishing* 36, no. 3 (2005): 129–132.

Gardner, Martin. *The Ambidextrous Universe.* London: Penguin, 1967.

Geertz, Clifford. *Works and Lives: The Anthropologist as Author.* Stanford: Stanford University Press, 1988.

Gegeo, David Welchman. "Cultural Rapture and Indigeneity: The Challenge of (Re)visioning 'Place' in the Pacific." *Contemporary Pacific* 13, no. 2 (2001): 491–507.

Gegeo, David Welchman, and Karen Ann Watson-Gegeo. "Whose Knowledge? Epistemological Collisions in Solomon Islands Community Development." *Contemporary Pacific* 14, no. 2 (2002): 377–409.

Genette, Gérard. *Paratexts: Thresholds of Interpretation.* Translated by Jane E. Lewin. Cambridge: Cambridge University Press, 1997.

Goldbort, Robert. *Writing for Science.* New Haven, CT: Yale University Press, 2006.

Goodrich, Peter. "Satirical Legal Studies: From the Legists to the Lizard." *Michigan Law Review* 103, no. 3 (2004): 397–517.

Gowers, Ernest. *The Complete Plain Words.* 2nd ed. London: Her Majesty's Stationery Office, 1973.

Grafton, Anthony. *The Footnote: A Curious History.* Cambridge, MA: Harvard University Press, 1997.

Green, David. "New Academics' Perceptions of the Language of Teaching and Learning: Identifying and Overcoming Linguistic Barriers." *International Journal for Academic Development* 14, no. 1 (2009): 33–45.

Greenblatt, Stephen. "Racial Memory and Literary History," *PMLA* 116, no. 1 (2001): 48–63.

———. "Writing as Performance: Revealing 'The Calculation That Underlies the Appearance of Effortlessness.'" *Harvard Magazine*, September /October 2007, 40–47.

Grey, Christopher, and Amanda Sinclair. "Writing Differently." *Organization* 13, no. 3 (2006): 443–453.

Guest, David E., and Neil Conway. "Communicating the Psychological Contract: An Employer Perspective." *Human Resource Management Journal* 12, no. 2 (2002): 22–38.

Harrison, Robert Pogue. *Forests: The Shadow of Civilization.* Chicago: University of Chicago Press, 1992.

Harte, John. *Consider a Spherical Cow: A Course in Environmental Problem Solving.* Sausalito, CA: University Science Books, 1988.

Hartley, James. "To Attract or to Inform?" *Journal of Technical Writing and Communication* 35, no. 2 (2005): 203–213.

Heilbron, John L. "Bohr's First Theories of the Atom." *Physics Today* 38, no. 10 (1985): 28–36.

———. *The Sun in the Church: Cathedrals as Solar Observatories.* Cambridge, MA: Harvard University Press, 1999.

Henige, David. "Discouraging Verification: Citation Practices across the Disciplines." *Journal of Scholarly Publishing* 37, no. 2 (2006): 99–118.

Henley, Margaret. "'Throwing a Sheep' at Marshall McLuhan." Paper presented at the Tertiary Education Research in New Zealand (TERNZ) Conference, Auckland, November 2007.

Hofstadter, Douglas R. *Gödel, Escher, Bach: An Eternal Golden Braid.* 20th anniv. ed. New York: Basic Books, 1999.

———. *Metamagical Themas: Questing for the Essence of Mind and Pattern.* New York: Basic Books, 1985.

Hofstadter, Douglas R., and David Moser. "To Err Is Human; To Study Error-Making Is Cognitive Science." *Michigan Quarterly Review* 27, no. 2 (1989): 185–193.

Humphreys, Glyn W., and M. Jane Riddoch. "How to Define an Object: Evidence from the Effects of Action on Perception and Attention." *Mind and Language* 22, no. 5 (2007): 534–547.

Hyland, Ken. *Disciplinary Discourses: Social Interactions in Academic Writing.* Ann Arbor: University of Michigan Press, 2004.

———. "Humble Servants of the Discipline? Self-Mention in Research Articles." *English for Specific Purposes* 20, no. 3 (2001): 207–226.

Kaplan, E. Ann. *Trauma Culture: The Politics of Terror and Loss in Media and Literature.* New Brunswick, NJ: Rutgers University Press, 2005.

Kelly, Frances. "Writing in the Frame-Lock." Paper presented at the Writing Research across Borders Conference, Santa Barbara, CA, February 2008.

Kerr, Clark. *The Uses of the University.* Cambridge, MA: Harvard University Press, 1963.

Knish, Anne [Arthur Davison Ficke], and Emanuel Morgan [Witter Bynner]. *Spectra: A Book of Poetic Experiments.* New York: Mitchell Kennerley, 1926.

Kováč, Ladislav. "Science and September 11th: A Lesson in Relevance." *World Futures: The Journal of General Evolution* 59, no. 5 (2003): 319–334.

Kreber, Carolin, ed. *The University and Its Disciplines: Teaching and Learning within and beyond Disciplinary Boundaries.* New York and London: Routledge, 2009.

Lakoff, George, and Mark Johnson. *Metaphors We Live By.* Chicago: University of Chicago Press, 1981.

———. *Philosophy in the Flesh: The Embodied Mind and Its Challenge to Western Thought.* New York: Basic Books, 1999.

Lämmel, R., and S. P. Jones. "Scrap Your Boilerplate: A Practical Design Pattern for Generic Programming." *ACM SIGPLAN Notices* 38, no. 3 (2003): 26–37.

Lamont, Michèle. *How Professors Think: Inside the Curious World of Academic Judgment.* Cambridge, MA: Harvard University Press, 2009.

Land, Ray, and Siân Bayne, "Screen or Monitor? Issues of Surveillance and Disciplinary Power in Online Learning Environments." In *Education in Cyberspace,* edited by Ray Land and Siân Bayne, 165–178. Abingdon, UK: RoutledgeFalmer, 2005.

Lanham, Richard A. *Revising Prose,* 3rd ed. New York: Macmillan, 1992.

Limerick, Patricia Nelson. "Dancing with Professors: The Trouble with Academic Prose." *New York Times Book Review,* October 31, 1993, 23–24.

Lindley, S., P. Wadler, and J. Yallop. "Idioms Are Oblivious, Arrows Are Meticulous, Monads Are Promiscuous." Paper presented at the Mathematically Structured Functional Programming workshop, Iceland, 2008.

MacLeish, Archibald. "Ars Poetica." In *Collected Poems, 1917–1982.* Boston: Houghton Mifflin, 1985.

Madigan, Robert, Susan Johnson, and Patricia Linton. "The Language of Psychology: APA Style as Epistemology." *American Psychologist* 4, no. 6 (1995): 428–436.

Mailloux, Steven. *Disciplinary Identities: Rhetorical Paths of English, Speech, and Composition.* New York: Modern Languages Association, 2006.

Marlow, S., and S. P. Jones. "Making a Fast Curry: Push/Enter vs. Eval/ Apply for Higher-Order Languages." *Journal of Functional Programming* 16, nos. 4–5 (2006): 415–449.

Marsh, Selina Tusitala. "Theory 'versus' Pacific Island Writing: Toward a Tama'ita'i Criticism in the Works of Three Pacific Island Woman Poets." In *Inside Out: Literature, Cultural Politics, and Identity in the New Pacific,* edited by Vilsoni Hereniko and Rob Wilson, 337–356. Lanham, MD: Rowman and Littlefield, 1999.

McGrath, Charles. "J. D. Salinger, Author Who Fled Fame, Dies at 91 (Obituary)." *New York Times,* January 29, 2010.

Mermin, Nathaniel David. "The Amazing Many-Colored Relativity Engine." *American Journal of Physics* 56, no. 7 (July 1988): 600–611.

———. "Copenhagen Computation: How I Learned to Stop Worrying and Love Bohr." *IBM Journal of Research and Development* 48, no. 1 (January 2004): 53–61.

———. "From Cbits to Qbits: Teaching Computer Scientists Quantum Mechanics." *American Journal of Physics* 71, no. 1 (January 2003): 23–30.

Merriam-Webster Collegiate Dictionary. 11th ed. Springfield, MA: Merriam-Webster, 2003.

Mogck, Brian David. *Writing to Reason: A Companion for Philosophy Students and Instructors.* Oxford: Blackwell, 2008.

Nabokov, Vladimir. *Pale Fire.* New York: Random House, 1989.

Nash, Robert J. *Liberating Scholarly Writing: The Power of Personal Narrative.* New York: Teachers College Press, 2004.

Norris, Ken, Adrian Freeman, and Julian F. V. Vincent. "The Economics of Getting High: Decisions Made by Common Gulls Dropping their Cockles to Open Them." *Behaviour* 137, no. 6 (2000): 783–807.

Nygaard, Lynn P. *Writing for Scholars: A Practical Guide to Making Sense and Being Heard.* Oslo, Norway: Universitetsforlaget, 2008.

Odersky, M., E. Runne, and P. Wadler. "Two Ways to Bake your Pizza: Translating Parameterised Types into Java." Paper presented at the International Seminar on Generic Programming, Germany, 2000.

Orwell, George. "Politics and the English Language." In *All Art is Propaganda: Critical Essays,* 270–286. Compiled by George Packer. Orlando, FL: Harcourt, 2008.

Oxford English Dictionary. 2nd ed. 20 vols. Oxford: Clarendon Press, 1989.

Paivio, Allan. *Mental Representations: A Dual Coding Approach.* Oxford: Oxford University Press, 1984.

Pascoe, Judith. *The Sarah Siddons Audio Files: Romanticism and the Lost Voice.* Ann Arbor: University of Michigan Press, 2011.

Pearson, G. A., ed. *Why Children Die: A Pilot Study.* London: CEMACH, 2006.

Pelias, Robert J. *A Methodology of the Heart.* Walnut Creek, CA: AltaMira Press, 2004.

Peseta, Tai. "Troubling Our Desires for Research and Writing within the Academic Development Project." *International Journal for Academic Development* 12, no. 1 (2007): 15–23.

Pfeffer, Jeffrey, and Tanya Menon. "Valuing Internal vs. External Knowledge: Explaining the Preference for Outsiders." *Management Science* 49, no. 4 (2003): 497–513.

Pinker, Steven. "Words and Rules." *Lingua* 106 (1998): 219–242.

———. *Words and Rules: The Ingredients of Language.* London: Weidenfeld and Nicholson, 1999.

Poe, Edgar Allan. *The Telltale Heart and Other Writings.* New York: Bantam Books, 2004.

Pope, Rob. *Textual Intervention: Critical and Creative Strategies for Literary Studies.* London: Routledge, 1995.

Pullman, Philip. "From Exeter to Jordan." *Oxford Today: The University Magazine* 14, no. 3 (Trinity 2002): 3.

Pyne, Stephen J. *Voice and Vision: A Guide to Writing History and Other Serious Non-Fiction.* Cambridge, MA: Harvard University Press, 2009.

Rabinowitz, Harold, and Suzanne Vogel. *The Manual of Scientific Style: A Guide for Authors, Editors, and Researchers.* Amsterdam and Boston: Academic Press, 2009.

Richardson, Laurel. "Writing Strategies: Reaching Diverse Audiences." *Qualitative Research Methods* 21 (1990): 5–42.

Richerson, Peter J., and Robert Boyd. *Not by Genes Alone.* Chicago: University of Chicago Press, 2005.

Root-Bernstein, Robert S. "The Sciences and Arts Share a Common Creative Aesthetic." In *The Elusive Synthesis: Aesthetics and Science,* edited by Alfred I. Tauber, 49–82. Dordrecht, Netherlands: Kluwer, 1996.

Rosanoff, M. A. "Edison in His Laboratory." *Harper's Monthly Magazine,* vol. 165, June/November 1932, 402–417.

Rose, Gillian. "Family Photographs and Domestic Spacings: A Case Study." *Transactions of the Institute of British Geographers* 28, no. 1 (2003): 5–18.

Rosner, Victoria. *Modernism and the Architecture of Private Life*. New York: Columbia University Press, 2005.

Sacks, Oliver. *An Anthropologist on Mars: Seven Paradoxical Tales*. New York: Alfred A. Knopf, 1995.

———. *Awakenings*. New York: Doubleday, 1973.

———. *The Island of the Colorblind*. New York: Vintage, 1997.

———. *A Leg to Stand On*. New York: Touchstone, 1998.

———. *The Man Who Mistook His Wife for a Hat*. New York: Simon and Schuster, 1998.

———. *Musicophilia: Tales of Music and the Brain*. New York: Knopf, 2007.

———. "The Power of Music." *Brain* 129, no. 10 (2006): 2528–2532.

———. *Uncle Tungsten: Memories of a Chemical Boyhood*. New York: Knopf, 2001.

Salmond, Anne. "Their Body Is Different, Our Body Is Different: European and Tahitian Navigators in the 18th Century." *History and Anthropology* 16, no. 2 (2005): 167–186.

Schön, Donald A. *The Reflective Practitioner: How Professionals Think in Action*. New York: Basic Books, 1984.

Seuss, Dr. "The Zax." In *The Sneetches and Other Stories*, 25–35. London: Collins, 1984.

Shankweiler, Donald. "Words to Meanings." *Scientific Studies of Reading* 3, no. 2 (1999): 113–127.

Shulman, Lee. "Signature Pedagogies in the Professions." *Daedalus* 134, no. 3 (Summer 2005): 52–59.

Sokal, Alan. "A Physicist Experiments with Cultural Studies." *Lingua Franca* 4 (May 1996): 62–64.

———. "Transgressing the Boundaries: Towards a Transformative Hermeneutics of Quantum Gravity." *Social Text* 46/47 (Spring/Summer 1996): 217–252.

Sparkes, Andrew C. "Embodiment, Academics, and the Audit Culture: A Story Seeking Consideration." *Qualitative Research* 7, no. 4 (2007): 521–550.

Sternberg, Robert J. *Cupid's Arrow: The Course of Love through Time*. Cambridge: Cambridge University Press, 1998.

Strunk, William, Jr., and E. B. White. *The Elements of Style*, 4th ed. Needham Heights, MA: Allyn and Bacon, 2000.

Swales, John. *Genre Analysis: English in Academic and Research Settings*. Cambridge: Cambridge University Press, 1990.

Sword, Helen. *The Writer's Diet*. Auckland: Pearson Education New Zealand, 2007.

Thody, Angela. *Writing and Presenting Research.* London: Sage, 2006.

Thompson, Hunter S. *Fear and Loathing in Las Vegas: A Savage Journey to the Heart of the American Dream.* London: Flamingo, 1993.

Thyer, Bruce A. *Preparing Research Articles.* Oxford and New York: Oxford University Press, 2008.

Trowler, Paul. "Beyond Epistemological Essentialism: Academic Tribes in the Twenty-First Century." In *The University and Its Disciplines: Teaching and Learning within and beyond Disciplinary Boundaries,* edited by Carolin Kreber, 181–195. New York: Routledge, 2009.

Turley, Richard Marggraf. *Writing Essays: A Guide for Students in English and the Humanities.* New York: Routledge, 2000.

Twain, Mark. *The Adventures of Huckleberry Finn.* New York: C. L. Webster, 1885.

Ulansey, David. *The Origins of the Mithraic Mysteries: Cosmology and Salvation in the Ancient World.* Oxford: Oxford University Press, 1989.

Van Valen, Leigh. "A New Evolutionary Law." *Evolutionary Theory* 1 (1973): 1–30.

Vincent, Julian F. V. "If It's Tanned It Must Be Dry: A Critique." *Journal of Adhesion* 85, no. 11 (2009): 755–769.

Wadler, Philip. "Et tu, XML? The Downfall of the Relational Empire." Paper presented at the 27th Annual Conference on Very Large Databases (VLDB), Rome, Italy, 2001.

Wadler, Philip, and R. B. Findler. "Well-Typed Programs Can't Be Blamed." Paper presented at the European Symposium on Programming (ESOP), Budapest, Hungary, 2008.

Watson, J. D., and F. H. C. Crick. "A Structure for Deoxyribose Nucleic Acid." *Nature* 171, no. 4356 (1953): 737–738.

Webster, James. *Haydn's "Farewell Symphony" and the Idea of Classical Style: Through-Composition and Cyclic Integration in His Instrumental Music.* Cambridge: Cambridge University Press, 1991.

———. "Music, Pathology, Sexuality, Beethoven, Schubert." *Nineteenth Century Music* 17, no. 1 (1993): 83–93.

White, E. B. *Charlotte's Web.* London: Hamish Hamilton, 1952.

Williams, Joseph M. *Style: Lessons in Clarity and Grace,* 9th ed. New York: Pearson Longman, 2007.

Wise, Steve. "Revolution in References: Give Readers a Chance by Putting Page Numbers." *Nature* 408 (November 23, 2000): 204.

Wiseman, Richard. *Did You Spot the Gorilla? How to Recognise the Hidden Opportunities in Your Life.* London: Arrow Books, 2004.

Wolff, Jonathan. "Literary Boredom." *Guardian*, September 24, 2007.

Woolf, Virginia. *To the Lighthouse: The Original Holograph Draft.* Transcribed and edited by Susan Dick. London: Hogarth Press, 1982.

Zinsser, William. *On Writing Well: An Informal Guide to Writing Non-fiction.* New York: Harper and Row, 1980.

ACKNOWLEDGMENTS

During the past few years, I have had so many stimulating conversations about academic writing with so many colleagues in so many countries—Australia, Canada, England, Finland, France, Hungary, New Zealand, Scotland, South Africa, Spain, Sweden, and the United States—that I cannot possibly acknowledge them all here. To all the stylish writers and thinkers who have contributed their ideas, insights, and inspiring examples to this book, I extend my warm and grateful thanks.

For their thoughtful, eloquent, and in some cases voluminous responses to my initial e-mailed query about academic style: Elizabeth Anderson, Anita Arvast, Erik Borg, John Butcher, Bruce Calvert, Nicole Rege Colet, John Collins, Peter Cook, Wystan Curnow, Rob Cuthbert, Shirley Dow, John Dunn, Phil Edwards, Lewis Elton, Elizabeth Evans, Jenn Fishman, Susan Gray, Mike Hanne, Mark Hauber, Keith Hutchinson, Anna Janssen, Joce Jesson, Hester Joyce, Bill Kirton, Bridget Kool, Ernest Linsay, Brenda Lobb, Julia Lockheart, Heather MacKenzie, Maree McEntee, Julienne Molineaux, Nancy November, Boris Pavlov, Tai Peseta, Jim Phelan, Suzanne Phibbs, Terri Rees, Dory Reeves, Regula Schmid, Mano Singham, Greg Smith, Jan Smith, Lynn Sorenson, Fritha Stalker, Veronica Strang, Eluned Summers-Bremner, Barbara Thomborson, Sue Tickner, Rolf Turner, Anne Wealleans, Benjamin D. Watanabe Williams, Bill Wolff, and Michael Wright.

For unsolicited feedback of the kind that keeps a writer nourished in times of famine: Debra Anstis, Amani Bell, Graham Bradley, John Brooks, Kelly Coate, Joan Appleton Costanza, Sara Cotterall, Vivienne Elizabeth, James Hartley, Isabeau Iqbal, Darryn Joseph, Meha Pare, Tepora Pukepuke, Pip Rhodes, Chris Smaill, and Angela Thody.

For their collegiality, adventurousness, and scholarly devotion to engaging academic writing: Brenda Allen, Satya Amirapu, Olga Filippova, Fabiana Kubke, Manuel Oyson, Wayne Stewart, and Yvonne Sun.

For generous financial support: The Centre for Academic Development, the Faculty of Education, and the Research Office at the University of Auckland.

For designing the graphics in Chapters 2 and 3: Tony Chung.

For permission to reproduce the diagram in Chapter 9 (from Elizabeth J. Allan, Suzanne P. Gordon, and Susan V. Iverson, "Re/thinking Practices of Power: The Discursive Framing of Leadership in the 'Chronicle of Higher Education,'" *Review of Higher Education* 30, no. 1, p. 49, Fig. 1, © 2006 by the Association for the Study of Higher Education): The Johns Hopkins University Press.

For permission to reproduce the Virginia Woolf drawing in Chapter 11: The Society of Authors as the Literary Representative of the Estate of Virginia Woolf.

For allowing me to expand on ideas originally explored in my article, "Writing Higher Education Differently: A Manifesto on Style" (*Studies in Higher Education* 34, no. 3, May 2009: 319–336): Taylor and Francis Ltd., http://www.informaworld.com.

For various forms of help, advice, encouragement, and succor along the way: Amit Bansal, Julie Bartlett-Trafford, Bill Barton, Adam Blake, Marion Blumenstein, Godfrey Boehnke, Brian Boyd, Ian Brailsford, Linda Bryder, Susan Carter, Alison Cleland, Michael Corballis, Hamish Cowan, Jan Cronin, Santanu Das, Ashwini Datt, Claire Donald, Sam Elworthy, Peter Gossman, Barbara Grant, Cameron Grant, Russell Gray, David Green, Cathy Gunn, Penny Hacker, Neil Haigh, Meegan Hall, John Hamer, Tony Harland,

Lynette Herrero-Torres, Matthew Hill, Kaye Hodge, Wen-Chen Hol, Craig Housley, Marjorie Howes, Barry Hughes, Hilary Janks, Alison Jones, Frances Kelly, Barbara Kensington-Miller, Te Kani Kingi, Michele Leggott, Andrea Lunsford, Fran Lyon, Robyn Manuel, Selina Tusitala Marsh, Christiane Maurer, Archie McGeorge, John Morrow, Kathryn Philipson, Elizabeth Ramsay, Matiu Ratima, Ray Ryan, Kimberly Brown Seely, Tessa Sillifant, Karen Springen, Lorraine Stefani, Hugh Stevens, Sean Sturm, Kathryn Sutherland, Kate Thomson, Malcolm Tight, Jacquie True, Demetres Tryphonopoulos, Lesley Wheeler, Martin Wilkinson, Les Tumoana Williams, Katarina Winka, Gina Wisker, and the Scary Book Babes.

For hour upon hour of meticulous research assistance: Hannah Field, Alison Hunt, Gregory Kan, Caroline Sturgess, and especially Louisa Shen.

For their faith in this book when it was little more than a gleam in its author's eye: my energetic agent, John W. Wright, and my wise editor, Elizabeth Knoll.

And finally, for their patience, good humor, and love: my children, Claire, Peter, and David, and my amazing husband, Richard Sorrenson, who makes everything possible.

INDEX